PRAYERS OF LIFE

MICHEL QUOIST

Translated by
ANNE MARIE DE COMMAILE
and
AGNES MITCHELL FORSYTH

GILL AND MACMILLAN

Published by
GILL AND MACMILLAN LTD.
2 BELVEDERE PLACE
DUBLIN I
and in London
through association with the
MACMILLAN
Group of Publishing Companies

SBN 7171 0158 4 *Paper edition*
SBN 7171 0159 2 *Rexine edition*

Printing history:
15   14   13   12   11

Grateful acknowledgement
is made to the Oxford University Press
and the Cambridge University Press
for permission to quote extracts from
the *New English Bible—New Testament*
(Copyright 1961, Oxford and
Cambridge University Presses) and to the
Cardinal Archbishop of Westminster
& Burns & Oates Ltd for extracts
from Monsignor R. A. Knox's translation
of the *Holy Bible*

Cover designed by Roisin Daly

Printed in Great Britain by Richard Clay (The Chaucer Press), Ltd.,
Bungay, Suffolk

Contents

CONTENTS

To pray these pages

Before being written these pages were both lived and prayed. They stem from the lives of committed Christians offered to God day by day. We record these experiences to help others to bring to God every aspect of their lives and to transfigure their lives through prayer. All the facts mentioned here are authentic.

These pages can hardly be used as "set prayers" in the usual sense. They are meditations on life, and should help Christians to discover the riches of a contact with God arising from the daily events of their existence. But they must not make us neglect liturgy and the words which were first put on our lips by Christ himself, and then by the Church.

God is always the initiator in his dialogue with man. That is why, in the first chapters, we have attempted to speak for God, as Péguy did before us.

But very soon the Christian must do more than imagine what God is saying to him; he must listen to him actually speaking in his life and in the world. God addresses us through every event, even the most insignificant. Very short prayers, of which we have given a few samples, may help us to meet the Lord at every step on our road.

Yet, it is not only when we are active that we must turn to God. We must learn to be still before him and talk over our lives fully with him—like a child who has been away for a while and returns to tell his father in detail of all his doings. Some of our longer prayers describe this intimate sharing with our Father, beginning with an object, a person, an event, and throwing the light of faith on some part of our everyday life. Those who take the trouble to meditate before God will realize that in these prayers there is a constant call to give ourselves to men, our brothers. Wherever the Father has placed us, we must live and fight that his kingdom of love and justice may come. This is not a matter of choice; it is the very meaning of our Christian life.

Some Christians may be disturbed by certain of these prayers. We beg them to be courageous enough not to skip over the troublesome pages, not to shut off the questions which, through them, God asks. It is better to listen to God beckoning to us in this life, than to hear him condemning us in the next.

Prayer often reveals the extent of our self-giving to others and of our friendship with Christ. We have grouped together prayers which, we hope, will enlighten Christians on their road—obscure at times—toward total self-giving.

Furthermore, to those who love the God who has surrendered himself for them, an essential part of their response is to follow him on his way to Calvary. However, we have suffered too much from (and sometimes smiled at) the well-worn phrases of our parents' "Stations of the Cross" not to attempt re-writing them very simply here. We know that our words also will quickly lose their force. Never mind. The cut flower fades, but others grow.

Naturally, one should not read this book as one would a novel. Purposely varied, these prayers are meant to answer the problems that the Christian encounters and help him to weave them into his prayer.

Finally, we have prefaced the prayers with texts of Scripture, to give the Christian—if he did not have it already—the inclination to meditate the Gospel and to find in it his daily nourishment. Thus are united here, supplementing each other, the Gospel and life, the two channels through which God speaks to men.

May those who read these pages hear God and answer him. In writing them, we hope for one thing only: to open the way for the amazing dialogue between man and his God.

MICHEL QUOIST

Le Havre, 18 June 1954

PRAYERS OF LIFE

If we knew
how to listen to God

*If we knew how to listen to God, we should hear him
speaking to us. For God does speak. He speaks in his
Gospel; he speaks also through life—that new Gospel to which
we ourselves add a page each day. But because our
faith is too weak and our life too earth-bound,
we are rarely open to God's message. To help us to listen,
at the beginning of our new intimacy with Christ,
let us imagine what he would say if he himself interpreted
his Gospel for the men of our day.*

I like youngsters

They brought children for him to touch; and the disciples scolded them for it. But when Jesus saw this he was indignant, and said to them, Let the children come to me; do not try to stop them; for the kingdom of God belongs to such as these. I tell you, whoever does not accept the kingdom of God like a child will never enter it. (Mark, 10, 13-15)

God says: I like youngsters. I want people to be like them.
I don't like old people unless they are still children.
I want only children in my kingdom; this has been decreed from
    the beginning of time.
Youngsters—twisted, humped, wrinkled, white-bearded—all
    kinds of youngsters, but youngsters.
There is no changing it, it has been decided, there is room for
    no one else.
I like little children because my likeness has not yet been dulled
    in them.
They have not botched my likeness, they are new, pure, without
    a blot, without a smear.
So, when I gently lean over them, I recognize myself in them.
I like them because they are still growing, they are still im-
    proving.
They are on the road, they are on their way.
But with grown-ups there is nothing to expect any more.
They will no longer grow, no longer improve.
They have come to a full stop.

It is disastrous—grown-ups think they have arrived.

I like youngsters because they are still struggling, because they
    are still sinning.
Not because they sin—if you understand me—but because they
    know that they sin, and they say so, and they try not to
    sin any more.

But I don't like grown-ups, they never harm anyone, they have
nothing to reproach themselves for.
I can't forgive them, I have nothing to forgive.
It is a pity, it is indeed a pity, because it is not true.

But above all, I like youngsters because of the look in their
eyes. In their eyes I can read their age.
In my heaven, there will be only five-year-old eyes, for I know
of nothing more beautiful than the pure eyes of a child.
It is not surprising, for I live in children, and it is I who look
out through their eyes.
When pure eyes meet yours, it is I who smile at you through
the flesh.
But on the other hand, I know of nothing sadder than lifeless
eyes in the face of a child.
The windows are open, but the house is empty.
Two eyes are there, but no light.
And, saddened, I stand at the door, and wait in the cold and
knock. I am eager to get in.
And he, the child, is alone.
He fattens, he hardens, he dries up, he gets old. Poor old
fellow!

Alleluia! Alleluia! Open, all of you, little old men!
It is I, your God, the Eternal, risen from the dead, coming to
bring back to life the child in you.
Hurry! Now is the time. I am ready to give you again the
beautiful face of a child, the beautiful eyes of a child . . .
For I love youngsters, and I want everyone to be like them.

Son,
I beseech you, don't sleep
any more

We must contemplate Christ on the way to Calvary. We must relive with him the Stations of his Cross to become deeply aware of his love for us. But his Passion is not fully completed. Lived by the Christ who assumed all the sins and sufferings of men two thousand years ago, it is now relived in the world, and will be till the end of time. Christ, living in his members, continues to suffer and die for us under our eyes. The Way of the Cross winds through our towns and cities, our hospitals and factories, and through our battlefields; it takes the road of poverty and suffering in every form.

It is in front of these new Stations of the Cross that we must stop and meditate and pray to the suffering Christ for strength to love him enough to act.

It is now my happiness to suffer for you. This is my way of helping to complete, in my poor human flesh, the full tale of Christ's afflictions still to be endured, for the sake of his body which is the church. (Col. 1, 24)

"I shall be in agony till the end of time," God says.
I shall be crucified till the end of time.
My sons the Christians don't seem to realize it.
I am scourged, buffeted, stretched out, crucified; I die in front
    of them and they don't know it, they see nothing, they
    are blind.
They are not true Christians, or they would not go on living
    while I am dying.

Lord, I don't understand; it is not possible; you exaggerate.
I would defend you if you were attacked.
I would be at your side if you were dying.
Lord, I love you!

5

That is not true, God says. Men are deluding themselves.

They say they love me, they believe they love me, and, as I
    am willing to admit, they are often sincere, but they are
    terribly mistaken. They do not understand, they do not see.

Slowly everything has been distorted, dried up, emptied.

They think they love me because once a month they honour my
    Sacred Heart.

As if I loved them only twelve times a year!

They think they love me because they keep to their devotions
    regularly, attend a benediction, eat fish on Fridays, burn
    a candle or say a prayer before a picture of my Sacred
    Heart.

But I am not made of plaster, God says, nor of stone nor of
    bronze.

I am living flesh, throbbing, suffering.

I am among men, and they have not recognized me.

I am poorly paid, I am unemployed, I live in a slum, I have
    tuberculosis, I sleep under bridges, I am in prison, I am
    oppressed, I am patronized.

And yet I said to them: "Whatever you do to my brothers,
    however humble, you do to me". . . . That's clear.

The worst is that they know it, but that they don't take it
    seriously.

They have broken my heart, God says, and I have waited for
    someone to have pity on me, but no one has.

I am cold, God says, I am hungry, I am naked.

I am imprisoned, laughed at, humiliated.

But this is a minor passion, for men have invented more terrible
    ordeals.

Armed with their liberty, formidably armed with their liberty,

They have invented . . .

"Father, forgive them; they do not know what they are doing."

They have invented war, true war.

And they have invented the Passion.

For I am everywhere that men are, God says,

Since the day when I slipped among them, on a mission, to save
    them all.

Since the day when I definitely committed myself to trying to
    gather them together.

6

Now I am rich and I am poor, a workman and a boss.

I am a Union member and a non-Union member, a striker and a strike-breaker, for men, alas! make me do all kinds of things.

I am on the side of the demonstrators and on the side of the police, for men, alas! transform me into a policeman.

I am a leftist, a rightist and even in the centre.

I am this side of the Iron Curtain and beyond.

I am a German and a Frenchman, a Russian and an American,

A Chinese from Nationalist China and one from Communist China,

I am from Vietnam and from Vietminh.

I am everywhere men are, God says.

They have accepted me, they possess me, the traitors!

Hail, Master!

And now I am with them, one of them, their very selves.

Now, see what they have done to me . . .

They are scourging me, crucifying me,

They tear me apart when they tear at one another.

They kill me when they kill one another.

Men have invented war . . .

I jump on mines, I gasp my last breath in foxholes,

I moan, riddled with shrapnel; I collapse under the volley of machine-gun fire,

I sweat men's blood on all battlefields,

I cry out in the night and die in the solitude of battle.

O world of strife, immense cross on which, every day, men stretch me.

Wasn't the wood of Golgotha enough?

Was this immense altar necessary for my sacrifice of love?

While around me men keep on shouting, singing, dancing, and, as if insane, crucify me in an enormous burst of laughter.

Lord, enough! Have pity on me!

Not that! it isn't I!

Yes, son, it is you.

You, and your brothers, for

several blows are needed to drive in a nail,

several lashes are needed to furrow a shoulder,

several thorns are needed to make a crown,
and you belong to the humanity that all together condemns
me.
It matters not whether you are among those who hit or among
those who watch, among those who perform or among those
who let it happen.
You are all guilty, actors and spectators.
But above all, son, don't be one of those who are asleep, one
of those who can still fall asleep . . . in peace. Sleep!
Sleep is terrible!
"Can you not watch one hour with me?"

On your knees, son! Do you not hear the roar of battle?
The bell is ringing,
Mass is starting,
God is dying for you, crucified by men.

If only we knew how to look at life

If only we knew how to look at life as God sees it,
we should realize that nothing is secular in the world,
but that everything contributes to the building of the kingdom
of God. To have faith is not only to raise
one's eyes to God to contemplate him; it is also to look at
this world—but with Christ's eyes.
If we had allowed Christ to penetrate our whole being,
if we had purified ourselves, the world would no longer
be an obstacle, it would be a perpetual incentive
to work for the Father in order that, in Christ,
his kingdom might come on earth as it is in heaven.
We must pray to have sufficient faith to know how to look at life.

I would like to rise very high

Praise be to the God and father of our Lord Jesus Christ, who has bestowed on us in Christ every spiritual blessing in the heavenly realms. In Christ he chose us before the world was founded, to be dedicated, to be without blemish in his sight, to be full of love; and he destined us—such was his will and pleasure—to be accepted as his sons through Jesus Christ. (Eph. 1, 3-5) He has made known to us his hidden purpose—such was his will and pleasure determined beforehand in Christ—to be put into effect when the time was ripe; namely, that the universe, all in heaven and on earth, might be brought into a unity in Christ. (Eph. 1, 9-10)

I would like to rise very high, Lord,
Above my city
Above the world
Above time.
I would like to purify my glance and borrow your eyes.

I would then see the universe, humanity, history, as the Father
    sees them.
I would see in the prodigious transformation of matter,
In the perpetual seething of life,
Your great body that is born of the breath of the Spirit.
I would see the beautiful, the eternal thought of your Father's
    love taking form step by step,
Everything summed up in you, things on earth and things in
    heaven.
And I would see that today, like yesterday, the most minute
    details are part of it.
Every man in his place.
Every group
And every object.
I would see a factory, a theatre, collective bargaining and the
    construction of a fountain.

I would see a crowd of youngsters going to a dance,
A baby being born, and an old man dying.
I would see the tiniest particle of matter and the smallest throbbing
of life,
Love and hate,
Sin and grace.
Startled, I would understand that the great adventure of love,
which started at the beginning of the world, is unfolding
before me,
The divine story which, according to your promise, will be
completed only in glory after the resurrection of the flesh,
When you will come before the Father, saying: All is accomplish-
ed, I am Alpha and Omega, the Beginning and the End.
I would understand that everything is linked together,
That all is but a single movement of the whole of humanity
and of the whole universe towards the Trinity, in you, by
you, Lord.
I would understand that nothing is secular, neither things, nor
people, nor events,
But that, on the contrary, everything has been made sacred in
its origin by God
And that everything must be consecrated by man made divine.
I would understand that my life, an imperceptible breath in this
great whole,
Is an indispensable treasure in the Father's plan.
Then, falling on my knees, I would admire, Lord, the mystery
of this world
Which, in spite of the innumerable and hateful snags of sin,
Is a long throb of love, towards love eternal.

I would like to rise very high, Lord,
Above my city
Above the world
Above time.
I would like to purify my glance and borrow your eyes.

All life
would become a sign

If we knew how to look at life through God's eyes,
we should see it as innumerable tokens of the love of the Creator
seeking the love of his creatures. The Father has put
us into the world, not to walk through it with lowered eyes,
but to search for him through things, events, people.
Everything must reveal God to us.
Long prayers are not needed in order to smile at Christ
in the smallest details of daily life.
The following lines intend to give a few simple examples
of the manifestations of his love.

The Telephone

I have just hung up; why did he telephone?
I don't know ... Oh! I get it ...
I talked a lot and listened very little.

Forgive me, Lord, it was a monologue and not a dialogue.
I explained my idea and did not get his;
Since I didn't listen, I learned nothing,
Since I didn't listen, I didn't help,
Since I didn't listen, we didn't communicate.

Forgive me, Lord, for we were connected,
and now we are cut off.

Green Blackboards

The school is up-to-date.
Proudly, the principal tells of all the improvements.
The finest discovery, Lord, is the green blackboard.
The scientists have studied long, they have made experiments;
We know now that green is the ideal colour, that it doesn't tire the eyes, that it is quieting and relaxing.

It has occurred to me, Lord, that you didn't wait so long to paint the trees and the meadows green.
Your research laboratories were efficient, and in order not to tire us, you perfected a number of shades of green for your modern meadows.
And so the "finds" of men consist in discovering what you have known from time immemorial.
Thank you, Lord, for being the good Father who gives his children the joy of discovering by themselves the treasures of his intelligence and love,
But keep us from believing that—by ourselves—we have invented anything at all.

The Wire-fence

The wires are holding hands around the holes;
To avoid breaking the ring, they hold tight the neighbouring
 wrist,
And it's thus that with holes they make a fence.

Lord, there are lots of holes in my life.
There are some in the lives of my neighbours.
But if you wish we shall hold hands
We shall hold very tight
And together we shall make a fine roll of fence to adorn Paradise.

My Friend

I shook hands with my friend, Lord,
And suddenly when I saw his sad and anxious face, I feared that
 you were not in his heart.
I am troubled as I am before a closed tabernacle when there is
 no light to show that you are there.
If you were not there, Lord, my friend and I would be separated.
For his hand in mine would be only flesh in flesh
And his love for me that of man for man.
I want your life for him as well as for me.
For it is only in you that he can be my brother.

The Brick

The bricklayer laid a brick on the bed of cement.
Then, with a precise stroke of his trowel spread another layer
And without a by-your-leave, laid on another brick.
The foundations grew visibly,
The building rose, tall and strong, to shelter men.

I thought, Lord, of that brick buried in the darkness at the base
    of the big building.
No one sees it, but it accomplishes its task, and the other bricks
    need it.
Lord, what difference whether I am on the roof-top or in the
    foundations of your building, as long as I stand faithfully at
    the right place?

Posters

They are loud.
I cannot avoid them, for they crowd together on the wall,
    alluring and tempting.
Their violent colours hurt my eyes
And I can't rid myself of their distasteful presence.

Lord, in the same way too often I draw attention to myself.
Grant that I may be more humble and unobtrusive,
And above all keep me from trying to impress others through
    showy display,
For it is your light only, Lord, that must draw all men.

The Underground

The last ones squeeze in.
The door rolls shut.
The train rumbles off.
I can't move.
I am no longer an individual, but a crowd,
A crowd that moves in one piece like jellied soup in its tin.

A nameless and indifferent crowd, probably far from you, Lord.
I am one with the crowd, and I see why it's sometimes hard for
    me to rise higher.
This crowd is heavy—leaden soles on my feet, my slow feet—
    a crowd too large for my overburdened skiff.
Yet, Lord, I have no right to overlook these people, they are
    my brothers,
And I cannot save myself, alone.

Lord, since you wish it, I shall make for heaven in the Under-
    ground.

The Swing

He was gently swinging at the end of the ropes.
Eyes shut, relaxed and drifting, he listened to the murmur of the
    breeze that sang a lullaby as it swayed him back and forth.
And minutes floated away to the rhythm of the swing.

So, Lord, I walk through the city as through a vast county fair,
    and see men drifting, blown by the breezes of life.
Some smile, and yield to passing pleasures.
Others with taut faces curse the wind that shakes them and
    knocks them into one another.

Lord, I want them to stand up on their swings,
I want them to grasp the cords that you hold out to them.
I want them to harden their muscles and brace their vigorous
    bodies, and stamp on their lives the direction they have
    chosen.
For you do not want your sons to drift,
But to live.

At The Door

The boy stumbled on the doorstep and the door slammed behind
   him.
He was punished.
Suddenly aware of his disgrace, he rushed in anger at the unfeeling
   door.
He slapped it, pounded it, stamping and shrieking.
But not a fibre moved on the wooden surface.
The boy caught sight of the key-hole—ironic eye of that sullen
   door—
But on peering into it he saw that it was blocked.
Then, in despair, he sat down and cried.

I watched him smiling, and realized, Lord, that often I exhaust
   myself before locked doors.
I want to make my points, persuade, prove,
And I talk and brandish arguments,
I strike hard to reach the imagination or the emotions,
But I am politely or violently dismissed—I waste my strength,
   vain fool that I am.

Grant me, Lord, to be respectful and patient,
Loving and praying in silence,
Standing at the door till it is opened.

All of life
would become prayer

If we knew how to listen to God, if we knew
how to look around us, our whole life would become prayer.
For it unfolds under God's eyes and no part of it must be
lived without being freely offered to him.
At first we communicate with God through words
which may be dispensed with later on.
Let us then make use of the following pages, but soon discard
words, as one does the peelings of a fruit.
Words are only a means.
However, the silent prayer which has moved
beyond words must always spring from everyday life,
for everyday life is the raw material of prayer.

Prayer
before a Five Pound Note

We can hardly respect money enough for the blood and toil it represents.
Money is frightening. It can serve or destroy man.

Corruption has fallen on your riches; all the fine clothes are left moth-eaten and the gold and silver have long lain rusting. That rust will bear witness against you . . . You have kept back the pay of the workmen who reaped your lands, and it is there to cry out against you; the lord of hosts has listened to their complaint. (James 5, 2-4, Knox)
Sell what you have, and give alms so providing yourselves with a purse that time cannot wear holes in, an inexhaustible treasure laid up in heaven, where no thief comes near, no moth consumes. Where your treasure-house is, there your heart is too. (Luke 12, 33-34, Knox)

Lord, see this note, it frightens me.
You know its secrets, you know its history.
How heavy it is!
It scares me, for it cannot speak.
It will never tell all it hides in its creases.
It will never reveal all the struggles and efforts it represents, all the disillusionment and slighted dignity.
It is stained with sweat and blood.
It is laden with all the weight of the human toil which makes its worth.

It is heavy, heavy, Lord.
It fills me with awe, it frightens me.
For it has death on its conscience,
All the poor fellows who killed themselves for it . . .
To possess it for a few hours,
To have through it a little pleasure, a little joy, a little life . . .

23

Through how many hands has it passed, Lord?
And what has it done in the course of its long, silent trips?

It has offered white roses to the radiant fiancée.
It has paid for the baptismal party, and fed the growing baby.
It has provided bread for the family table.
Because of it there was laughter among the young, and joy
    among the adults.
It has paid for the saving visit of the doctor,
It has bought the book that taught the youngster,
It has clothed the young girl.

But it has sent the letter breaking the engagement.
It has paid for the death of a child in its mother's womb.
It has bought the liquor that made the drunkard.
It has produced the film unfit for children.
And has recorded the indecent song.
It has broken the morals of the adolescent and made of the adult
    a thief.
It has bought for a few hours the body of a woman.
It has paid for the weapons of the crime and for the wood of the
    coffin.

O Lord, I offer you this note with its joyous mysteries, its
    sorrowful mysteries.
I thank you for all the life and joy it has given.
I ask your forgiveness for the harm it has done.
But above all, Lord, I offer it to you as a symbol of all the labours
    of men, indestructible money, which tomorrow will be
    changed into your eternal life.

The Pornographic
Magazine

The body is matter, but is God's creation, and spirit ennobles it.
The body of a Christian who is conscious of God's life in him
becomes the temple of the Holy Spirit and a member of Christ.
Hence its dignity. When it is neglected or scoffed at, God himself is
insulted.

*Surely you know that you are God's temple, where the spirit of God
dwells. Anyone who destroys God's temple will himself be destroyed by
God, because the temple of God is holy; and that temple you are.*
(I Cor. 3, 16-17)

*Anyone who loves me will heed what I say; then my father will love him,
and we will come to him and make our dwelling with him.* (John 14, 23)

Now you are Christ's body, and each of you a limb or organ of it. (I Cor.
12, 27)

*I will unfold a mystery: . . . we shall all be changed in a flash . . . and
the dead will rise immortal.* (I Cor. 15, 51-52)

So the word became flesh. (John 1, 14)

Lord, I am ashamed of this magazine.
You must be profoundly hurt in your infinite purity.

The office workers all contributed to buy it.
The boy ran to fetch it.

And pored over it on the way back.
Here it is.
On its shining pages, naked bodies are exposed,
Going from office to office, from hand to hand;
Such foolish giggles, such lustful glances . . .
Empty bodies, soulless bodies,
Adult toys for the hardened and the soiled.

And yet, Lord, man's body *is* beautiful.
From the beginning you, the supreme Artist, held the model
before you, knowing that one day you would dwell in a
human body when taking on the nature of man.
Slowly you shaped it with your powerful hands; and into its
inert matter you breathed a living soul.
From then on, Lord, you asked us to respect the body, for the
whole body is a conveyor of the spirit,
And we need this sensitive instrument that our spirits may
commune with those of our brothers.

Words, in long processions, lead us toward other souls.
A smile on our lips, the expression in our eyes, reveal the soul.
The clasp of a hand carries it to a friend,
A kiss yields it to the loved one,
The embrace of the couple unites two souls in quest of a new
child of God.

But it was not enough for you, Lord, to make of our flesh the
visible sign of the spirit.
Through your grace the Christian's body became sacred, and the
temple of the Trinity.
A member of the Lord, and a bearer of his God,
Supreme dignity of this splendid body!

Here, Lord, before you, tonight, are the bodies of sleeping men:

The pure body of the tiny child,
The soiled body of the prostitute,
The vigorous body of the athlete,
The exhausted body of the factory worker,
The soft body of the playboy,
The surfeited body of the rich man,

The starved body of the poor man,
The neglected body of the slum child,
The feverish body of the sick man,
The painful body of the injured man,
The paralyzed body of the cripple,
    All bodies, Lord, of all ages.

Here is the body of the fragile new-born baby, plucked like ripe
    fruit from its mother.
Here is the body of the light-hearted child who falls and gets
    up, unmindful of his bruises.
Here is the body of the worried adolescent who doesn't know
    that it's a fine thing to grow up.
Here is the body of the grown man, powerful and proud of his
    strength.
Here is the body of the old man, gradually failing.

I offer them all to you, Lord, and I ask you to bless them, while
    they lie in silence, wrapped in your night.
Left by their sleeping souls, they are there before your eyes, your
    own.
Tomorrow, shaken from their sleep, they will have to resume
    work.
May they be servants and not masters,
Welcoming homes and not prisons,
Temples of the living God, and not tombs.
May these bodies be developed, purified, transfigured by those
    who dwell in them,
And may we find them, at the end of their days, faithful com-
    panions, illumined by the beauty of their souls.

In your sight, Lord, and in your Mother's,
Since you both belong to our earth,
All the bodies of men will be guests in glory of your eternal
    heaven.

The Tractor

Machines are a means of progress if, by greatly increasing man's strength, they serve him. Unfortunately, too often man is a slave to their rhythmic beat and power. Machines are the servants of profit, but man is the servant of machines. We must struggle to re-establish a balance. As man extends himself and becomes more powerful through machines he should also develop his spirit, rise above his mechanical work, master it and offer it to God.

Whatever you are doing, whether you speak or act, do everything in the name of the Lord Jesus, giving thanks to God the father through him. (Col. 3, 17)

I don't like tractors, Lord.
I saw one in a field a while ago,
And I loathed it.

Tractors are conceited.
They crush man with all their strength.
They never look at him, they just move forward,
But when they move forward, they crawl, and *that* pleases me.

They are ugly,
They move clumsily, shaking their heavy frames.
Their silly noses upturned, panting,
Coughing their deep, measured, mechanical cough.
But they are stronger than man, Lord.
Regularly, imperturbably, they pull their load;
They pull what a hundred human arms could not move,
They carry what a hundred human hands could not lift.
A tractor is ugly, yet it is strong, and I need it.
But it needs me, it needs man.

It needs man to exist, it is man who made it.

It needs man to move, it is man who starts it going.

It needs man to go forward, it is man who steers it.

It needs man, especially, that it may be consecrated.

For a tractor has no soul, Lord, and it is man who must lend it his own.

I offer you tonight, Lord, the work of all the tractors in the country, of all the tractors in the world.

I offer you the efforts of all the machines that have no soul with which to offer themselves.

I pray that they shall not crush man with their haughty power, but rather that they shall serve him;

I pray that man, in the freedom of his soul, shall dominate them,

And thus praise you by their work, glorify you,

And share in creation's solemn mass which is said every day through human labour, and will be said till the end.

The Funeral

For a Christian, death does not exist, or, rather, it is only a starting-point and not an end. The Church sings at funerals: 'Life is not taken away, it is changed,'[1] and the anniversary of the death of the blessed it calls a 'birth-day.' St Thérèse of Lisieux, on her death-bed, murmured, 'I am not dying, I am entering into life.'
Our dead are alive, and unless they are condemned forever, we can find them again in God. If we wish to live eternally with them, we must meet with Christ, listen to him and commune with him.

I am the resurrection and I am life. (John 11, 25)
In very truth I tell you, if anyone obeys my teaching he shall never know what it is to die. (John 8, 51)
I am that living bread . . . if anyone eats this bread he shall live for ever. (John 6, 51)
Now if this is what we proclaim, that Christ was raised from the dead, how can some of you say there is no resurrection of the dead? . . . if Christ was not raised, then our gospel is null and void, and so is your faith . . . if it is for this life only that Christ has given us hope, we of all men are most to be pitied. (I Cor. 15, 12-14-19)

People were following:
The family—some crying,
Some pretending to cry;
Friends—some grieving,
Some bored or chatting.

Leaving the cemetery, some of the family were sobbing: "All is finished."
Others were sniffling: "Come, come, my dear, courage, it's finished!"

[1] Preface to the Mass of the Dead.

Some friends murmured: "Poor man, that's how we'll all finish."
And others sighed in relief: "Well, it's over."

And I was thinking that everything was just beginning.

Yes, he had finished the last rehearsal, but the eternal show was
    just beginning.
The years of training were over, but the eternal work was about
    to commence.
He had just been born to life,
The real life,
Life that's going to last,
Life eternal.

As if there were dead people!
There are no dead people, Lord.
There are only the living, on earth and beyond.
Death is real, Lord,
But it's nothing but a moment,
A second, a step,
The step from provisional to permanent,
From temporal to eternal.
So in the death of the child the adolescent is born,
    from the caterpillar emerges the butterfly,
    from the grain the full-blown ear.

Death, grotesque character, bogey-man of little children, non-
    existent phantom,
I don't take you seriously,
But I am disgusted with you.
You terrify the world,
You frighten and deceive men,
And yet your only reason for existing is life, and you are not
    able to take from us those that we love.

But where are they, Lord, those that I have loved?
Are they in ecstasy, taken up with holy loving in harmony with
    the Trinity?
Are they tormented in the night, burning with desire to love
    with an infinite love?
Are they in despair, condemned to their own selves because they

preferred themselves to others? Consumed with hate because they can no longer love?

Lord, my loved ones are near me.
I know that they live in the shadow.
My eyes can't see them because they have left for a moment their bodies as one leaves behind outmoded clothing.
Their souls, deprived of their disguise, no longer communicate with me.

But in you, Lord, I hear them calling me.
I see them beckoning to me.
I hear them giving me advice.
For they are now more vividly present.
Before, our bodies touched but not our souls.
Now I meet them when I meet you.
I receive them when I receive you.
I love them when I love you.
O, my loved ones, eternally alive, who live in me,
Help me to learn thoroughly in this short life how to live eternally.

Lord, I love you, and I want to love you more.
It's you who make love eternal, and I want to love eternally.

The Sea

Lives that are effective are not always those that attract attention. They are never those of the proud who storm against obstacles which cannot be removed. Lives lived humbly, under the eyes of God, illumined by his grace and radiant with love for others, are always effective.

Love is patient; love is kind and envies no one. Love is never boastful, nor conceited, nor rude; never selfish, nor quick to take offence. Love keeps no score of wrongs; does not gloat over other men's sins, but delights in the truth. There is nothing love cannot face; there is no limit to its faith, its hope, and its endurance. (I Cor. 13, 4-7)

Lord, I saw the sea attacking the rocks, sombre and raging.
From afar the waves gained momentum.
High and proud, they leapt, jostling one another to be the first to strike.
When the white foam drew back, leaving the rock clear, they gathered themselves to rush forward again.

The other day I saw the sea, calm and serene.
The waves came from afar, creeping, not to draw attention.
Quietly holding hands, they slipped noiselessly and stretched at full length on the sand, to touch the shore with the tips of their beautiful, soft fingers.
The sun gently caressed them, and they generously returned streams of light.

Lord, grant that I may avoid useless quarrels that tire and wound without achieving results.
Keep me from these angry outbursts that draw attention but leave one uselessly weakened.

Keep me from wanting always to outstrip others in my conceit, crushing those in my way.

Wipe from my face the look of dark, dominating anger.

Rather, Lord, grant that I may live my days calmly and fully, as the sea slowly covers the whole shore.

Make me humble like the sea, as, silently and gently, it spreads out, unnoticed.

May I wait for my brothers and match my pace to theirs, that I may move upward with them.

Grant me the triumphant perseverance of the waters.

May each of my retreats turn into an advance.

Give my face the light of clear waters.

Give my soul the whiteness of foam.

Illumine my life that it may sing like sunbeams on the surface of the sea.

But above all, Lord, may I not keep this light for myself, and may all those who come near me return home eager to bathe in your eternal grace.

Eyes

Man's eyes have great power, for they are conveyors of the soul. When God dwells in a man, his eyes can carry God to men.

As he was starting out on a journey, a stranger ran up, and, kneeling before him, asked, 'Good Master, what must I do to win eternal life?' Jesus said to him, '... You know the commandments: Do not murder;...' 'But, Master,' he replied, 'I have kept all these since I was a boy.' Jesus looked straight at him; his heart warmed to him, and he said, 'One thing you lack: go, sell everything you have, ... and come, follow me.' (Mark 10, 17-21) A serving-maid who saw (Peter) sitting in the firelight stared at him and said, 'This man was with him too.' But he denied it: 'Woman,' he said, 'I do not know him.' ... At that moment, while he was still speaking, a cock crew; and the Lord turned and looked straight at Peter. And Peter remembered the Lord's words, ... He went outside, and wept bitterly. (Luke 22, 56-57, 60-62)
When he came in sight of the city, (Jesus) wept over it and said, 'If only you had known, on this great day, the way that leads to peace!' (Luke 19, 41-42)
(Andrew) brought Simon to Jesus, who looked him in the face, and said, 'You are Simon, son of John. You shall be called Cephas.' (John 1, 42)
The lamp of the body is the eye. If your eyes are sound, you will have light for your whole body; if the eyes are bad, your whole body will be in darkness. (Matt. 6, 22)

I am now about to close my eyelids, Lord,
For my eyes this evening have finished their work
And will return home,
Having walked for a day in the garden of men.
Thank you, Lord, for my eyes, windows open on the wide world;
Thank you for their look that carries my soul as the broad sun-
    beam carries the light and warmth of your sun.

I pray to you during the night, that, tomorrow, when I open my
    eyes to the clear morning,
They shall be ready to serve both my soul and my God.
May my eyes be clear and straightforward, Lord, and give others
    a hunger for purity;
May my look never be one of disappointment,
                       disillusionment,
                       despair;
But may it know how to admire,
                  contemplate,
                  adore.
May my eyes learn to close in order to find you more easily;
But may they never turn away from the world because they are
    afraid.
May my eyes be penetrating enough to recognize your presence
    in the world,
And may they never shut on the afflictions of men.

May my eyes be firm and steady,
But may they also know how to soften in pity and be capable of
    tears.
May my gaze not soil the one it touches,
May it not disturb, but may it bring peace.
May it not sadden, but rather may it transmit joy.
May it not attract in order to hold captive,
But rather may it persuade others to rise above themselves to you.
May my eyes disquiet the sinner because in them he will see
    your light,
But may their reproach lead to encouragement.
Grant that my eyes may be startling because they are an encounter,
    an encounter with God.
Grant that they be a call,
    a clarion call,
        that brings all the world to its doorstep,
Not because of me, Lord,
But because you are to pass by.
That my eyes may be all this, Lord,
Once more, this evening,
I give you my soul,
I give you my body,
I give you my eyes,

That in looking at men, my brothers,
It may be you who look at them
And you who beckon.

To Love—
The Prayer
of the Adolescent

Adolescence is not the 'silly age,' it is the splendid age, the age when God, through the laws of nature, puts in the young person's body and heart a deep call towards a body other than his own, towards a heart other than his own.

May every young person then have someone to explain this to him, parents who love him enough not to cling to him selfishly, but to direct his attention to the new and clear road along which 'she' will appear.

May he have a friend, a brother, who will help him to forget himself for others, lest he become a slave to himself, incapable of loving.

We for our part have crossed over from death to life; this we know, because we love our brothers. The man who does not love is still in the realm of death . . . It is by this that we know what love is: that Christ laid down his life for us. And we in our turn are bound to lay down our lives for our brothers. (I John 3, 14, 16)

Dear friends, let us love one another, because love is from God . . . but the unloving know nothing of God. For God is love. (I John 4, 7-8)

I want to love, Lord,
I need to love.
All my being is desire;
My heart,
My body,
      yearn in the night towards an unknown one to love.
My arms thrash about and I can seize on no object for my love.
I am alone and want to be two.
I speak, and no one is there to listen.

I live, and no one is there to share my life.
Why be so rich and have no one to enrich?
Where does this love come from?
Where is it going?
I want to love, Lord,
I need to love.
Here this evening, Lord, is all my love, unused.

Listen, son,
Stop,
  and silently make a long pilgrimage to the bottom of your
  heart.
Walk by the side of your love so new, as one follows a brook to
  find its source,
And at the very end, deep within you, in the infinite mystery of
  your troubled soul, it is I whom you will meet,
For I call myself Love, son,
And from the beginning I have been nothing but love,
And love is in you.
It is I who made you to love,
To love eternally;
And your love will pass through another self of yours,
It is she that you seek;
Set your mind at rest, she is on your way,
  on the way since the beginning,
  the way of my love.
You must wait for her coming,
She is approaching,
You are approaching,
You will recognize each other,
For I've made her body for you, I've made yours for her.
I've made your heart for her, I've made hers for you,
And you seek each other, in the night,
In "my night," which will become Light, if you trust me.

Keep yourself for her, son,
As she is keeping herself for you.
I shall keep you for one another.
And, since you hunger for love, I've put on your way all your
  brothers to love.
Believe me, it's a long apprenticeship, learning to love,

And there are not several kinds of love:
Loving is always leaving oneself to go towards others . . .

Lord, help me to forget myself for others, my brothers,
That in giving myself I may teach myself to love.

I found Marcel alone

It is not easy to love, and if all too often our loves miscarry, isn't it because of a dreadful mistake? Were not our loves simply 'the clash of two egoisms'?[1] Did we even succeed in crossing the threshold of our own selves? If true love gives joy, it is bought by suffering.

... they are no longer two individuals: they are one flesh. What God has joined together, man must not separate. (Mark 10, 8-9)
... men also are bound to love their wives, as they love their own bodies. In loving his wife a man loves himself. For no one ever hated his own body: on the contrary, he provides and cares for it; and that is how Christ treats the church, because it is his body, of which we are living parts. Thus it is that (in the words of scripture) 'a man shall leave his father and mother and shall be joined to his wife, and the two shall become a single body.' It is a great truth that is hidden here. I for my part refer it to Christ and to the church, ... each of you must love his wife as his very self; and the woman must see to it that she pays her husband all respect. (Eph. 5, 28-33)

It was about noon when I knocked at his door.
I found Marcel alone, still lying on the bed which was now too
    big for him;
His wife had left him a few days ago.
It hurt me, Lord, to see that poor fellow so discouraged, that
    house half empty.
A presence was lacking,
A love was lacking.
I missed the bunch of flowers on the mantelpiece, the powder
    and lipstick on the wash-basin, the cloth on the table and
    the chairs properly arranged.

---

[1] Van der Meersch in *Corps et Ames.*

I found the dirty sheets on a bed wrinkled like an old face, the
    ash-trays filled to overflowing, shoes scattered on the floor,
    opened packages here and there, a rag on the arm-chair and
    the blinds closed.
It was dark, dismal, and stuffy.

It hurt me, Lord.
I felt something torn,
        something unbalanced,
Like a mechanism gone wrong,
Like a man with broken bones.

And I reflected that what you had planned was good,
And that there can be no order and beauty, love and joy, outside
    your plan.

I pray to you tonight, Lord,
        for Marcel and . . . for her
        and for the other one
        and for the wife of the other one
        and for his children
        and for the families involved
        and for the neighbours who gossip
        and for the colleagues who judge.

I ask of you forgiveness
        for all these lacerations,
        for all these wounds,
        and for your blood poured out, because of these wounds
        in your Mystical Body.

I pray to you tonight, Lord, for myself and for all my friends.
Teach us to love.

It is not easy to love, son.
Often when you think you love, it is only yourself that you love,
    and you spoil everything, you ruin everything.

To love is to meet oneself, and to meet oneself one must be
    willing to leave oneself and go towards another.

To love is to commune, and to commune one must forget oneself
　　for another,
One must die to self completely for another.
Loving hurts, you know, son,
For since the Fall—listen carefully, son—to love is to crucify
　　self for another.

The Delinquent

Man is alone, since he is unique, but he is made for communion. Sin divides and isolates us. We must grow closer, share the burden of each other's sins, and atone for them, to overcome the obstacle to our oneness. Solitude causes suffering; it is not part of the Father's plan. Redemptive love alone can conquer it and cement our unity.

A man was on his way from Jerusalem down to Jericho when he fell in with robbers, who stripped him, beat him, and went off leaving him half dead. It so happened that a priest was going down by the same road; but when he saw him, he went past on the other side. So too a Levite came to the place, and when he saw him went past on the other side. But a Samaritan who was making the journey came upon him, and when he saw him was moved to pity. He went up and bandaged his wounds, bathing them with oil and wine. Then he lifted him on to his own beast, brought him to an inn, and looked after him there. Next day he produced two silver pieces and gave them to the innkeeper, and said, 'Look after him; and if you spend any more, I will repay you on my way back.'
(Luke 10, 30-35)

I know his secret,
His weighty secret.
How, Lord, can it be carried by this big boy with the childish
    face grown old too soon?

I wanted him to tell it to me,
To give it to me to bear with him.
For long months now I have been stretching my hand towards
    this young, crushed brother.
Eagerly he seizes that hand, caresses it, kisses it . . . but over
    the gulf that separates us.
When I want to draw him gently closer, he backs away, for in

his other hand he carries his secret, too heavy for him to hand to me.

Lord, he hurts me.

I look at him from a distance, and cannot get near him,

He looks at me and cannot come closer.

We both suffer.

He suffers the most, and I can hardly bear it, for my love is too limited, Lord, and each time that I try to span his solitude, my bridge is too short and does not touch his shore.

And I see him, on the edge of his suffering, hesitating, getting set, but drawing back again in desperation, for the distance is too great and the burden is too heavy.

Yesterday, Lord, he leaned towards me, said a word—then took it back; his whole body quivered with the weight of the secret which approached his lips but rolled back again to the depths of his solitude.

He did not cry, but I wiped off big drops of perspiration beading his forehead.

I cannot take his burden from him, he must give it to me.

I see it, and I cannot grasp it.

You do not want me to take it, Lord, since he does not want that.

I have no right to violate his suffering.

I am thinking tonight, Lord, of all the isolated ones:

Of all those who are alone, utterly alone,

Because they have never let go and been carried by anyone,

Because they have never given themselves to you, Lord;

Those who know something that others will never know;

Those who suffer from a sore that no one can ever tend;

Those who bleed from a wound that no one will ever heal;

Those who are scarred by a vicious blow that no one will ever suspect;

Those who have, locked in the terrifying silence of their hearts, a harvest of humiliations, despairs, hatreds;

Those who have hidden a mortal sin—cold sepulchres behind cheerful fronts.

The solitude of man frightens me, Lord;

Every man is alone, since he is unique;

And that solitude is sacred; he alone can break through it, confide
and share confidences.
He alone can pass from solitude to communion.
And you want this communion, Lord. You want us to be united
with one another,
In spite of the deep gulf that we have dug between us by sin
you want us to be united as your Father and you are united.

Lord, that boy hurts me, as do all isolated ones.
Grant that I may love them enough to break through their
isolation.
Grant that I may pass through the world with all doors open,
My house entirely empty, available, welcoming.

Help me to withdraw so as to embarrass no one,
That others may come in without asking,
That they may deposit their burdens without being seen.
And I'll come, silently, to get them by night,
And you, Lord, will help me to bear them.

Thank you

We must know how to say Thank You. Our days are filled with the gifts the Lord showers on us. If we were in the habit of taking stock of them, at night we should be like a 'queen for a day,' dazzled and happy with so many blessings. We should then be grateful to God, secure because he gives us everything, joyful because we know that every day he will renew his gifts.

Everything is a gift from God, even the smallest things, and it's the sum of these gifts that makes a life beautiful or sad, depending on how we use them.

All good giving and every perfect gift comes from above, from the father of the lights of heaven. With him there is no variation, no play of passing shadows. (James 1, 17)

Thank you, Lord, thank you.
Thank you for all the gifts that you have given me today.
Thank you for all I have seen, heard, received.
Thank you for the water that woke me up,
　　　　　the soap that smells good,
　　　　　the tooth-paste that refreshes.
Thank you for the clothes that protect me, for their colour and
　　their style.
Thank you for the newspaper so faithfully there, for the comics,
　　my morning smile, for useful meetings, for justice done and
　　for big games won.
Thank you for the street-cleaning lorry and the men who run it,
　　for their morning shouts and all the early noises.
Thank you for my work, my tools, my efforts.
Thank you for the metal in my hands, for the whine of the steel
　　biting into it, for the satisfied look of the foreman and the
　　load of finished pieces.

Thank you for Jim who lent me his file, for Danny who gave me a cigarette, for Charlie who held the door for me.

Thank you for the welcoming street that led me there, for the shop windows, for the cars, for the passers-by, for all the life that flowed swiftly between the windowed walls of the houses.

Thank you for the food that sustained me, for the glass of beer that refreshed me.

Thank you for the car that meekly took me where I wanted to be, for the fuel that made it go, for the wind that caressed my face and for the trees that nodded to me on the way.

Thank you for the boy I watched playing on the footpath opposite,

Thank you for his roller-skates and for his comical face when he fell.

Thank you for the morning greetings I received, and for all the smiles.

Thank you for Mother who welcomes me at home, for her tactful affection, for her silent presence.

Thank you for the roof that shelters me, for the lamp that lights me, for the radio that plays, for the news, for music and singing.

Thank you for the bunch of flowers, so pretty on my table.

Thank you for the tranquil night.
Thank you for the stars.
Thank you for the silence.

Thank you for the time you have given me.
Thank you for life.
Thank you for grace.

Thank you for being there, Lord.
Thank you for listening to me, for taking me seriously, for gathering my gifts in your hands to offer them to your Father.
Thank you, Lord,
Thank you.

The Priest:
a prayer on Sunday night

People ask a great deal of their priest, and they are right. But they should understand that it is not easy to be a priest. He has given himself in all the ardour of youth, yet he still remains a man, and every day the man in him tries to take back what he has surrendered. It's a continual struggle to remain completely at the service of Christ and of others.

A priest needs no praise or embarrassing gifts; what he needs is that those committed to his charge should, by loving their fellows more and more, prove to him that he has not given his life in vain. And as he remains a man, he may need once in a while a delicate gesture of disinterested friendship . . . some Sunday night when he is alone.

Come with me, and I will make you fishers of men. (Mark 1, 17)
You did not choose me: I chose you. I appointed you to go on and bear fruit that shall last. (John 15, 16)
Forgetting what is behind me, and reaching out for that which lies ahead, I press towards the goal to win the prize which is God's call to the life above, in Christ Jesus. (Phil. 3, 13-14)

Tonight, Lord, I am alone.
Little by little the sounds died down in the church,
The people went away,
And I came home,
Alone.

I passed people who were returning from a walk.
I went by the cinema that was disgorging its crowd.
I skirted café terraces where tired strollers were trying to prolong
     the pleasure of a Sunday holiday.
I bumped into youngsters playing on the footpath,
Youngsters, Lord,

Other people's youngsters who will never be my own.

Here I am, Lord,
Alone.
The silence troubles me,
The solitude oppresses me.

Lord, I'm 35 years old,
A body made like others,
    ready for work,
A heart meant for love,
But I've given you all.
It's true, of course, that you needed it.
I've given you all, but it's hard, Lord.
It's hard to give one's body; it would like to give itself to others.
It's hard to love everyone and to claim no one.
It's hard to shake a hand and not want to retain it.
It's hard to inspire affection, to give it to you.
It's hard to be nothing to oneself in order to be everything to
    others.
It's hard to be like others, among others, and to be of them.
It's hard always to give without trying to receive.
It's hard to seek out others and to be unsought oneself.
It's hard to suffer from the sins of others, and yet be obliged to
    hear and bear them.
It's hard to be told secrets, and be unable to share them.
It's hard to carry others and never, even for a moment, be carried.
It's hard to sustain the feeble and never be able to lean on one who
    is strong.
It's hard to be alone,
Alone before everyone,
Alone before the world,
Alone before suffering,
        death,
        sin.

Son, you are not alone,
I am with you,
I am you.
For I needed another human vehicle to continue my Incarnation
    and my Redemption.

Out of all eternity, I chose you,
I need you.

I need your hands to continue to bless,
I need your lips to continue to speak,
I need your body to continue to suffer,
I need your heart to continue to love,
I need you to continue to save,
Stay with me, son.

Here I am, Lord;
Here is my body,
Here is my heart,
Here is my soul.
Grant that I may be big enough to reach the world,
Strong enough to carry it,
Pure enough to embrace it without wanting to keep it.
Grant that I may be a meeting-place, but a temporary one,
A road that does not end in itself, because everything to be
    gathered there, everything human, leads toward you.

Lord, tonight, while all is still and I feel sharply the sting of
    solitude,
While men devour my soul and I feel incapable of satisfying their
    hunger,
While the whole world presses on my shoulders with all its
    weight of misery and sin,
I repeat to you my "yes"—not in a burst of laughter, but slowly,
    clearly, humbly,
Alone, Lord, before you,
In the peace of the evening.

I spoke, Lord

Speech is God's gift. We shall have to account for it. It is through words that we communicate with each other and that we reveal what we are. We haven't the right to be silent, but speaking is a serious matter, and we must weigh our words in the sight of God.

I tell you this: there is not a thoughtless word that comes from men's lips but they will have to account for it on the day of judgement. For out of your own mouth you will be acquitted; out of your own mouth you will be condemned. (Matt. 12, 36-37)

Not everyone who calls me Lord, Lord will enter the kingdom of heaven, but only those who do the will of my heavenly father. When that day comes, many will say to me, Lord, Lord, did we not prophesy in your name, cast out devils in your name, and in your name perform many miracles? Then I will tell them to their face, I never knew you: out of my sight, you and your wicked ways! (Matt. 7, 21-23)

I spoke, Lord, and I am furious,
I am furious because I worked so hard with gestures and with
    words.
I threw my whole self into them, and I'm afraid the essential
    didn't get across.
For the essential is not mine, and words alone are too shallow to
    hold it.

I spoke, Lord, and I am worried.
I am afraid of speaking, for speaking is serious;
It's serious to disturb others, to bring them out, to keep them on
    their doorsteps;
It's serious to keep them waiting, with outstretched hands,

longing hearts, seeking for light or some courage to live and
act.
Suppose, Lord, that I should send them away, empty-handed!

And yet, I must speak.
You have given me speech for a few years, and I must make use of
it.
I owe my soul to others, and words are crowding to my lips to
bring it to them.
For the soul could not express itself if speech were taken from it.
We know nothing of the infant inside its little body,
And the whole family rejoices when, word by word, phrase by
phrase, its soul is revealed to them.
But when one of the family is dying, the others stand despairing
by his bed, listening intently to his last words.
He passes on, locked in silence, and his relatives will no longer
know his soul once they have shut his eyes and closed his lips.

Speech, Lord, is a gift, and I have no right to be quiet through
pride, cowardice, negligence or apathy.
Others have a right to my words, to my soul,
For I have a message to give them from you,
And none other than I, Lord, can give it to them.
I have something to say, short perhaps, but welling up from my
life, from which I cannot turn.
But my words must be true words.
It would be a breach of trust to seek the attention of another and
under the cover of words not reveal the truth of the soul.
The words that I pour out must be living words, full of the
mysteries that my unique soul has grasped, mysteries of the
world and of man.
The words that I speak must be conveyors of God, for the lips
that you have given me, Lord, are made to reveal my soul,
and my soul knows you and holds you close.
Forgive me, Lord, for having spoken so badly,
Forgive me for having spoken often to no purpose;
Forgive me for the days when I tarnished my lips with hollow
words,
false words,
cowardly words,
words through which you could not pass.

Uphold me when I must speak in a meeting, intervene in a
　　discussion, talk with a brother.
Grant above all, Lord, that my words may be like the sowing of
　　seeds,
And that those who hear them may look to a fine harvest.

That face, Lord, haunts
me

If we do not fight with all our strength, where the Father has placed us, against the world in disorder, we are not real Christians. We do not love God. For he said it through St John:

If he does not love the brother whom he has seen, it cannot be that he loves God whom he has not seen. (I John 4, 20)
My children, love must not be a matter of words or talk; it must be genuine, and show itself in action. (I John 3, 18)

But it isn't simply by improving the look of a man's face that a Christian can bring peace to his conscience; it is by finding and tackling all the social and moral disorders which have produced that face.
The poor will judge us.

And they too will reply, 'Lord, when was it that we saw you hungry or thirsty or a stranger or naked or ill or in prison, and did nothing for you?' And he will answer, 'I tell you this: anything you did not do for one of these, however humble, you did not do for me.' (Matt. 25, 44-45)

That face, Lord, has haunted me all evening.
It is a living reproach,
A prolonged cry that reaches me in my quietude.

That face is young, Lord, yet men's sins have struck it;
He was defenceless and exposed to their blows.

They came from all over;
Destitution came,

The shanty,
The dilapidated bed,
The foul air,
Smoke,
Alcohol,
Hunger,
The hospital,
The sanatorium.

Work—crushing, humiliating.
Unemployment,
The depression,
War.

Frenzied dances,
Revolting songs,
Demoralizing films,
Languorous music,
Unclean and deceitful kisses.

The struggle to live,
Rebellion,
Brawls,
Cries,
Blows,
Hate.

They came from everywhere,
Men with their horrid selfishness, their dreadful faces,
    their great, dirty fingers,
    their broken nails,
    their fetid breath.
They hastened here from the ends of the earth,
    from the bounds of time.
And slowly, one after another,
Or suddenly, all together, like brutes,
They struck,
    whipped,
    lashed,
    wrought,
    moulded,

              hammered,
              engraved,
              sculptured.
And here at last is this face, this poor face;
It took eighteen years to fashion it,
It took hundreds of centuries to produce it.
Ecce homo: behold the man.

Here is this poor face of a man, like an open book,
The book of the miseries and sins of men;
         the book of
                          selfishness,
                          conceit,
                          cowardice;
         the book of
                          greed,
                          lust,
                          abdications,
                          compromises.

Here it is like a mournful protest,
         like a cry of revolt,
              but also like a heart-rending call,
For behind this ridiculous, grimacing face,
Behind those uneasy eyes,
Like the clasped hands of one drowned, white on the dark surface
         of the pool,
Is a light,
A flame,
A tragic supplication,
The infinite desire of a soul to live above its mud.

Lord, that face haunts me, it frightens me, it condemns me;
For, with everyone else, I have made it, or allowed it to be made!
And I realize, Lord, that this boy is my brother, and yours.

What have we done with a member of your family?

I fear your judgement, Lord.
It seems to me that at the end of time all the faces of my brothers,
         and especially those of my town, my district, my work, will
         be lined up before me,

And in your merciless light I shall recognize in these faces
    the lines that I have cut,
    the mouth that I have twisted,
    the eyes that I have darkened,
    and those whose light I have extinguished.
They will come, those that I have known
    and those that I have not known,
    those of my time and all those that have followed,
    fashioned by the workshop of the world.
And I shall stand still, terrified, silent.
It is then, O Lord, that you will say to me
    . . . it was I . . .

Lord, forgive me for that face which has condemned me,
Lord, thank you for that face which has awakened me.

Hunger

All men are our brothers, for the blood of Christ made us sons of
the same Father. When a member of a family suffers and dies, the
other members grieve. Since we know now that millions of men
die of hunger in the world every year, we can no longer live as
before. Even if financial means permit, a mode of living other than
that which is fitting and necessary, is a sin—we repeat it again—it
is a sin to live without fighting with all our might, where we are,
for more justice in the world.

*There was once a rich man, who dressed in purple and the finest linen, and
feasted in great magnificence every day. At his gate, covered with sores,
lay a poor man named Lazarus, who would have been glad to satisfy his
hunger with the scraps from the rich man's table. Even the dogs used to
come and lick his sores.* (Luke 16, 19-21)

*He said to his disciples, Make them sit down . . . Then, taking the five
loaves and the two fishes, he looked up to heaven, said the blessing over
them, broke them, and gave them to the disciples to distribute to the
people. They all ate to their hearts' content.* (Luke 9, 14-17)

I have eaten,
I have eaten too much,
I have eaten only because others have done so,
Because I was invited,
Because I was in the world and the world would not have
    understood;
And each dish
And each mouthful
And each morsel was hard to get down.
I have eaten too much, Lord,

While at that moment, in my town, more than 1,500 persons
    queued up at the bread line,
While in her attic a woman ate what she had salvaged that
    morning from the garbage bins,
While urchins in their orphanage divided some scraps from the
    old folks' home.
While ten, a hundred, a thousand unfortunates throughout the
    world, at that very moment twisted in pain and died of
    hunger before their despairing families.

Lord, it's terrible, for I know,
Men know, now.

They know that not only a few destitute are hungry, but hundreds
    at their own doors.
They know that not only several hundreds but thousands are
    hungry on the borders of their country,
They know that not only thousands, but millions, are hungry
    throughout the world.

Men have made a map of the prevalence of hunger,
Areas of starvation and death, appalling.
The figures stand out in stark and implacable truth.
The minimum wage for a month here is, for millions and millions
    of human beings, their maximum wage for a year.
One third of humanity is underfed.
Several million die of hunger in India in the course of one famine
    alone.
On an average, the Indians live for barely 26 years.

Lord, you see this map, you read these figures,
Not like a calm statistician in his office,
But like the father of a large family bending over the head of
    each of his sons.
Lord, you have seen this map, you have read these figures since
    the beginning of time,
And you told the story, for me, of the rich man at table and the
    poor starved Lazarus;
And you spoke, for me, of the Last Judgement.
". . . I was hungry . . ."

It's you who queue up at the bread line,
It's you who eat the scraps of garbage,
It's you who are tortured by hunger and starve to death,
It's you who die alone in a corner at 26,
While in another corner of the great hall of the world—with
    some members of our family—I eat without being hungry,
    what is needed to save you.

" . . . I was hungry . . . "

Remind me of that, Lord, if I cease for a moment to give myself.
I'll never be through giving bread to my brothers, for there are
    too many of them.
There'll always be some who won't have had their share.
I'll never be through fighting to get bread for all my brothers.

Lord, it isn't easy to feed the world.
I would rather say my prayers regularly, properly;
I would rather fast on Fridays,
I would rather visit my poor man,
I would rather give to fêtes and orphanages;
But apparently that isn't enough.
It's nothing, if one day you can say to me: "I was hungry!"

Lord, I'm no longer hungry,
Lord, I don't want to be hungry again.
Lord, I want to eat only what I need to live, to serve you and
    to fight for my brothers.
For you are hungry, Lord,
You die of hunger, while I am surfeited.

Housing

The problem of housing, in the world's large cities, is appalling. It's our first duty to realize it. Many of the comfortably-housed have never even been through the slum quarters of their city. We must speak out, for public opinion is a powerful weapon, and each of us helps to create it. There are many organizations that need our active help, or, at the very least, our support. If we love our brothers, we shall always find a way, wherever we are, to do something for them.

Suppose a brother or a sister is in rags with not enough food for the day, and one of you says, Good luck to you, keep yourselves warm, and have plenty to eat, but does nothing to supply their bodily needs, what is the good of that? (James 2, 15-16)

Lord, I can't sleep; I have got up out of bed to pray.
It is night outside, and the wind blows and the rain falls,
And the lights of the city, signs of the living, pierce the darkness.
They bother me, Lord, these lights—why are you showing them
    to me?
They beckoned to me, and now they hold me captive, while
    the woes of the city murmur their muffled lament.
And I cannot escape them, Lord; I know these sufferings too well.
I see them rising before me,
I hear them speaking to me,
I feel them hitting me,
They were bothering me when I was trying to sleep.

I know that in one single room thirteen crowded people are
    breathing on one another.[1]
I know a mother who hooks the table and the chairs to the
    ceiling to make room for mattresses.

[1] All these facts are authentic. They were chosen among hundreds.

I know that rats come out to eat the crusts and bite the babies.
I know a father who gets up to stretch oil-cloth above the rain-soaked bed of his four children.
I know a mother who stays up all night since there is room for only one·bed, and the two children are sick.
I know a drunken father who vomits on the child sleeping beside him.
I know a big boy who runs away alone into the night because he can't stand it any more.
I know that some men fight for the women as there are three couples in the same attic.
I know a wife who avoids her husband as there is no room for another baby at home.
I know a child who is quietly dying, soon to join his four little brothers above.
I know . . .
I know hundreds of others—yet I was going to sleep peacefully between my clean-white sheets.

I wish I didn't know, Lord.
I wish it were not true.
I wish I could convince myself that I'm dreaming,
I wish someone could prove that I'm exaggerating,
I wish they'd show me that all these people are to blame, that it's their fault that they are so miserable.
I'd like to be reassured, Lord, but I can't, it's too late.
I've seen too much,
I've listened too much,
I've counted too much, and, Lord, these ruthless figures have robbed me forever of my innocent tranquillity.

So much the better, son,
For I, your God, your Father, am angry with you.
I gave you the world at the beginning of time, and I want each of my sons to have a home worthy of their Father, in my vast kingdom.
I trusted you, and your selfishness has spoiled everything.
It's one of your most serious sins, shared by many of you.
Woe unto you if, through your fault, a single one of my sons dies in body or in spirit.

I tell you, I will give to those the finest lodgings in Paradise. But the thoughtless, the negligent, the selfish, who, well sheltered on earth, have forgotten others, they have had their reward. There will be no room for them in my Kingdom.

Come, son, ask forgiveness for yourself and for others tonight. And tomorrow, fight with all your strength, for it hurts your Father to see that once more there is no room for his son at the inn.

The Hospital

Suffering is a mystery, and only faith can throw light on it. Pain is not willed by God. Men have rejected his plan; they have thrown man and the universe out of balance, and so suffering was born. But Christ came to straighten out the disorder. He made of useless suffering the very means of redemption.

Surely he hath borne our griefs, and carried our sorrows: yet we did esteem him stricken, smitten of God, and afflicted. But he was wounded for our transgressions, he was bruised for our iniquities: the chastisement of our peace was upon him; and with his stripes we are healed. (Isaiah 53, 4-5)

This afternoon I went to see a patient at the hospital.
From ward to ward I walked, through that city of suffering,
      sensing the tragedies hardly concealed by the brightly painted
      walls and the flower-bordered lawns.
I had to go through a ward; I walked on tiptoe, hunting for my
      patient.
My eyes passed quickly and discreetly over the sick, as one
      touches a wound delicately to avoid hurting.
I felt uncomfortable,
Like the uninitiated traveller lost in a mysterious temple,
Like a pagan in the nave of a church.
At the very end of the second ward I found my patient,
And once there, I could only stammer. I had nothing to say.

Lord, suffering disturbs me, oppresses me.
I don't understand why you allow it.
Why, Lord?
Why this innocent child who has been moaning for a week,
      horribly burned?

This man who has been dying for three days and three nights,
    calling for his mother?
This woman with cancer who in one month seems ten years
    older?
This worker fallen from his scaffolding, a broken puppet less than
    twenty years old?
This stranger, poor isolated wreck, who is one great open sore?
This woman in a cast, lying on a board for more than thirty years?
Why, Lord?
I don't understand.
Why this suffering in the World
        that shocks,
            isolates,
            revolts,
            shatters?
Why this hideous suffering that strikes blindly without seeming
    cause,
Falling unjustly on the good, and sparing the evil,
Which seems to withdraw, conquered by science, but comes
    back in another form, more powerful and more subtle?
I don't understand.
Suffering is odious and frightens me.
Why these people, Lord, and not others?
Why these, and not me?

Son, it is not I, your God, who has willed suffering, it is men.
They have brought it into the world in bringing sin,
Because sin is disorder, and disorder hurts.
There is for every sin, somewhere in the world and in time,
    a corresponding suffering.
And the more sins there are, the more suffering.

But I came, and I took all your sufferings upon me, as I took all
    your sins,
I took them and suffered them before you.
I transformed them, I made of them a treasure.
They are still an evil, but an evil with a purpose,
For through your sufferings, I accomplish redemption.

He was
in the middle of the street

The world is in such a state of disorder that many men, to earn their living, are forced to take part in work that destroys others, physically or morally. Victims of economic systems that are sinful, some are obliged to lie and to steal.

All those concerned should suffer profoundly from that tragic situation. They share the responsibility for the state of the world, and must recognize the sins of their society and blame themselves. But just as true contrition is found only when one seeks to change one's life, so true suffering for the sins of the social order is found only when one works to change systems that are inhuman. This is an absolute duty from which there is no dispensation for the Christian.

You are the light of the world; a city cannot be hidden if it is built on a mountain top. A lamp is not lighted to be put away under a bushel measure; it is put on the lamp-stand, to give light to all the people of the house; and your light must shine so brightly before men . . . (Matt. 5, 14-16; Knox)

He was in the middle of the street,
Staggering, and singing at the top of his lungs in the husky voice of a drunk.
People turned round and stopped, amused.
A policeman came silently from behind,
Grabbed him brutally by the shoulder, and took him to the police station.
He was still singing,
And people laughing.

I did not laugh, Lord.
I thought of his wife who would wait in vain for him that night.

I thought of all the other drunks of the town,
    those of the pubs and the bars,
    those of living-rooms and cocktail parties.
I thought of their home-coming, at night;
    of the frightened youngsters,
    the empty wallets,
    the blows,
    the cries,
    the tears,
I thought of the children who would be born of drunken
    embraces.

Now you have spread your night over the city, Lord,
And while tragedies unfold,
The men who have
                  justified alcohol,
                  produced alcohol,
                  sold alcohol,
That same night sleep in peace.
I think of all those men, and I pity them;
    they have produced and sold misery,
    they have produced and sold sin.
I think of all the others, the crowd of others who work
    to destroy and not to build,
    to stupefy and not to uplift,
    to debase and not to ennoble.
I think especially, Lord, of the many men who work for war,
    who, to feed a family, have to work to destroy others,
    who, to live, must manufacture death.
I don't ask you to keep them all from their work—that is not
    possible,
But, Lord,
    may they question it,
    may their sleep be uneasy,
    may they fight in this world of disorder,
    may they act as leaven,
    may they be redeemers.
By all the wounded in soul and body, victims of the work of their
    brothers,
By all the dead for whom thousands of men have conscientiously
    manufactured death,

By that drunk, grotesque clown in the middle of the street,
By the humiliation and tears of his wife,
By the fear and cries of his children,
Lord, have pity on me, too often slumbering.
Lord, have pity also on the miserable men who are completely
   asleep and collaborate in a world where brothers kill each
   other to earn their bread.

The Bald Head

We have been in God's thought from all eternity, and in his
creative love his attention never leaves us. We must see in our
brothers God's idea of them, and respect it. We must be attentive
to them even as God is attentive to us.

*In him (Christ) everything in heaven and on earth was created, not only
things visible but also the invisible . . . the whole universe· has been
created through him and for him. And he exists before everything, and all
things are held together in him.* (Col. 1, 16-17)
But not a hair of your head shall be lost. (Luke 21, 18)
*Are not sparrows five for twopence? And yet not one of them is overlooked
by God. More than that, even the hairs of your head have all been
counted. Have no fear; you are worth more than any number of sparrows.*
(Luke 12, 6-7)

For an hour it was before my eyes,
During the whole lecture.
That was a fine dome, Lord,
Polished, shining, girdled with a horse-shoe of hair carefully
      arranged and sternly held to the pattern prescribed.
The lecture bored me;
I had time to think,
And I thought, Lord, that you knew this dome well.
It hasn't been out of your sight for years, and every day you say
      yes, when old mother nature asks permission to take a few
      more hairs from the rapidly clearing field.
You said it in your Gospel; "Not one hair of your head falls
      without my permission."
It's true, Lord, that you are always thinking of us.
It's true, from the beginning of time, before we existed.

Even before the world existed,
You have been dreaming of me,
Thinking of me,
Loving me.
And it's true that your Love created me,
Not on an assembly-line, but unique,
The first one so made, and the last,
Indispensable to humanity.
It's true, Lord, that you have conceived for my life a unique
destiny.
It's true that you have an eternal plan for me alone,
A wonderful plan that you have always cherished in your heart,
as a father thinks over the smallest details in the life of his
little one still unborn.
It's true that, always bending over me, you guide me to bring
it about, light on my path and strength for my soul.
It's true that you are saddened when I stray or run away, but
that you hasten to pick me up if I stumble or fall.

Lord, you who make bald heads, but above all beautiful lives,
You, the divine Attentive One,
    the divine Patient One,
    the divine Present One,
See that at no time I forget your presence.
I don't ask you to bless what I myself have decided to do, but
give me the grace to discover and to live what you have
dreamed for me.
Lord, living in your grace, let me share a little, through the
attention I give to others, your loving care for us.
Let me, on my knees, adore in them the mystery of your creative
love.
Let me respect your idea of them without trying to impose my
own.
May I allow them to follow the path that you have marked out
for them without trying to take them along mine.
May I realize that they are indispensable to the world, and that I
can't do without the least among them.
May I never tire of looking at them and of enriching myself with
the treasures you have entrusted to them.
Help me to praise you in their journeying, to find you in their
lives.

And that not an instant of their existence should go by,
Not a hair of their heads fall,
By me as by you, unheeded.

Football at Night

Often men would rather be elsewhere, both in time and in space, than where they are, but this is a dangerous illusion. Each one is placed in the world in accordance with the Father's will for him. To make a success of one's life, and to help humanity to progress, one must take part in that life as fully as possible. That life is the work of the divine.

Some he has appointed to be apostles, others to be prophets, others to be evangelists, or pastors, or teachers. They are to order the lives of the faithful, minister to their needs, build up the frame of Christ's body, until we all realize our common unity through faith in the Son of God ... On him all the body depends; it is organized and unified by each contact with the source which supplies it; and thus, each limb receiving the active power it needs, it achieves its natural growth, building itself up through charity. (Eph. 4, 11-16, Knox)

This evening at the stadium the night was stirring, peopled with
ten thousand shadows.
And when the flood-lights had painted green the velvet of the
great field,
The night intoned a chorale, filled by ten thousand voices.

The master of ceremonies had given the signal to begin the
service.
The impressive liturgy moved forward smoothly.
The ball flew from celebrant to celebrant,
As if everything had been minutely planned in advance.
It passed from foot to foot, slipped along the field, and flew away
overhead.
Each was at his post, taking the ball in turn, passing it to the
next one who was there to receive and pass again.

73

And because each one did his part in the right place,
Because he put forth the effort required,
Because he knew he needed all the others,
Slowly but surely the ball gained ground
And made the final goal!

While, at the end, the immense crowd flowed laboriously into
    the narrow streets,
I reflected, Lord, that human history, for us a long game, is for
    you this great liturgy,
A prodigious ceremony initiated at the dawn of time, which
    will end only when the last celebrant has completed his final
    rite.

In this world, Lord, we each have our place.
You, the far-sighted coach, have planned it for us.
You need us here, our brothers need us, and we need everyone.

It isn't the position I hold that is important, Lord,
But the reality and strength of my presence.
What difference whether I am forward or back, as long as I am
    fully what I should be?

Here, Lord, is my day before me . . .
Did I sit too much on the side-lines, criticizing the play of others,
    my hands in my pockets?
Did I play my part well?
And when you were watching our side, did you see me there?
Did I catch my team-mate's pass and that of the player at the
    end of the field?
Did I co-operate with my team without seeking the limelight?
Did I play the game to obtain the victory, so that each one
    should have a part in it?
Did I battle to the end in spite of set-backs, blows and bruises?
Was I troubled by the demonstrations of the crowd and of the
    team, discouraged by their lack of understanding and their
    criticisms,
Made proud by their applause?
Did I think of praying my part, remembering that in the eyes
    of God this human game is the most religious of ceremonies?

I come in now to rest in the pavilion, Lord.
Tomorrow, if you kick off, I'll play a new position,
And so each day . . .
Grant that this game, played with all my brothers, may be the
    imposing liturgy that you expect of us,
So that when your last whistle interrupts our lives, we shall be
    chosen for the championship of heaven.

Lord, I have time

All men complain that they haven't enough time. It's because they look at their lives from too human a point of view. There's always time to do what God wants us to do, but we must put ourselves completely into each moment that he offers us.

Be most careful then how you conduct yourselves: like sensible men, not like simpletons. Use the present opportunity to the full, for these are evil days. So do not be fools, but try to understand what the will of the Lord is. (Eph. 5, 15-17)

I went out, Lord.
Men were coming out.
They were coming and going,
Walking and running.
Everything was rushing, cars, lorries, the street, the whole town.
Men were rushing not to waste time.
They were rushing after time,
To catch up with time,
To gain time.

Goodbye, sir, excuse me, I haven't time.
I'll come back, I can't wait, I haven't time.
I must end this letter—I haven't time.
I'd love to help you, but I haven't time.
I can't accept, having no time.
I can't think, I can't read, I'm swamped, I haven't time.
I'd like to pray, but I haven't time.

You understand, Lord, they simply haven't the time.
The child is playing, he hasn't time right now ... Later on ...
The schoolboy has his homework to do, he hasn't time ...

Later on . . .
The student has his courses, and so much work, he hasn't time . . .
Later on . . .
The young man is at his sports, he hasn't time . . . Later on . . .
The young married man has his new house, he has to fix it up,
     he hasn't time . . . Later on . . .
The grandparents have their grandchildren, they haven't time . . .
Later on . . .
They are ill, they have their treatments, they haven't time . . .
Later on . . .
They are dying, they have no . . .
Too late! . . . They have no more time!

And so all men run after time, Lord.
They pass through life running—hurried, jostled, overburdened,
     frantic, and they never get there. They haven't time.
In spite of all their efforts they're still short of time,
     of a great deal of time.
Lord, you must have made a mistake in your calculations.
There is a big mistake somewhere.
The hours are too short,
The days are too short,
Our lives are too short.

You who are beyond time, Lord, you smile to see us fighting it.
And you know what you are doing.
You make no mistakes in your distribution of time to men.
You give each one time to do what you want him to do.

But we must not lose time
          waste time,
          kill time,
For time is a gift that you give us,
But a perishable gift,
A gift that does not keep.

Lord, I have time,
I have plenty of time,
All the time that you give me,
The years of my life,
The days of my years,

The hours of my days,
They are all mine.
Mine to fill, quietly, calmly,
But to fill completely, up to the brim,
To offer them to you, that of their insipid water
You may make a rich wine such as you made once in Cana of
Galilee.

I am not asking you tonight, Lord, for time to do this and then
that,
But your grace to do conscientiously, in the time that you give
me, what you want me to do.

There are two loves only

We are made by love and for love. On earth we learn to love. At death we shall take our examination on love. If we have trained ourselves well enough, we shall go and live eternally in Love. Now here below every time that we love ourselves (selfishness) we fail a little in carrying out God's plan for us and for the world. There are but two loves, love of ourselves and love of God and of others.

To live is to choose between these two loves.

No servant can be slave to two masters; for either he will hate the first and love the second, or he will be devoted to the first and think nothing of the second. (Matt. 4, 24)

Only the man who loves his brother dwells in light: there is nothing to make him stumble. But one who hates his brother is in darkness; he walks in the dark and has no idea where he is going, because the darkness has made him blind. (I John 2, 10-11)

There are two loves only, Lord,
Love of myself and love of you and of others,
And each time that I love myself, it's a little less love for you
    and for others,
It's a draining away of love,
It's a loss of love,
For love is made to leave self and fly towards others.
Each time it's diverted to myself, it withers, rots and dies.
Love of self, Lord, is a poison that I absorb each day;
Love of self offers me a cigarette and gives none to my neighbour;
Love of self chooses the best part and keeps the best place;
Love of self indulges my senses and supplies them from the table
    of others;

Love of self speaks about myself and makes me deaf to the words of others;

Love of self chooses, and forces that choice on a friend;

Love of self puts on a false front, it wants me to shine, overshadowing others;

Love of self is self-pitying and overlooks the suffering of others;

Love of self advertises my ideas and despises those of others;

Love of self thinks me virtuous, it calls me a good man;

Love of self induces me to earn money, to spend it for my pleasure, to save it for my future;

Love of self advises me to give to the poor in order to ease my conscience and live in peace;

Love of self puts my slippers on and ensconces me in an easy chair;

Love of self is satisfied with myself, it gently rocks me to sleep.

What is more serious, Lord, is that love of self is a stolen love.

It was destined for others, they needed it to live, to thrive, and I have diverted it.

So the love of self creates human suffering,

So the love of men for themselves creates human misery,

All the miseries of men,

All the sufferings of men:

The suffering of the boy whose mother has slapped him without cause, and that of the man whose boss has reprimanded him in front of the other workers;

The suffering of the ugly girl neglected at a dance, and that of the woman whose husband doesn't kiss her any more;

The suffering of the child left at home because he's a nuisance, and that of the grandfather made fun of because he's too old;

The suffering of the worried man who hasn't been able to confide in anyone, and that of the troubled adolescent whose worries have been ridiculed;

The suffering of the desperate man who jumps into the canal, and that of the criminal who is going to be executed;

The suffering of the unemployed man who wants to work, and that of the worker who ruins his health for a ridiculous wage;

The suffering of the father who has to pile his family into a single room next to an empty house, and that of the mother whose children are hungry while the remains of someone's party are thrown into the dustbin;

The suffering of one who dies alone, while his family, in the adjoining room, wait for his death, drinking coffee.
All sufferings,
All injustices, bitternesses, humiliations, griefs, hates, despairs,
All sufferings are an unappeased hunger,
A hunger for love.
So men have built, slowly, selfishness by selfishness, a disfigured world that crushes them;
So men on earth spend their time feeding their self-love,
While around them others with outstretched arms die of hunger.
They have squandered love.
I have squandered your Love, Lord.

Tonight I ask you to help me to love.

Grant me, Lord, to spread true love in the world.
Grant that by me and by your children it may penetrate a little into all circles, all societies, all economic and political systems, all laws, all contracts, all rulings;
Grant that it may penetrate into offices, factories, apartment buildings, cinemas, dance-halls;
Grant that it may penetrate the hearts of men and that I may never forget that the battle for a better world is a battle of love, in the service of love.

Help me to love, Lord,
not to waste my powers of love,
to love myself less and less in order to love others more and more,
That around me, no one should suffer or die because I have stolen the love they needed to live.

Son, you will never succeed in putting enough love into the heart of man and into the world,
For man and the world are hungry for an infinite love,
And God alone can love with a boundless love.
But if you want, son, I give you my life,
Draw it within you.
I give you my heart, I give it to my sons.
Love with my heart, son,
And all together you will feed the world, and you will save it.

All

The Gospel preached in its utter purity exalts, frightens or shocks.
It is bound to meet with violent reactions, as it is diametrically
opposed to sinful man and to the 'world.' When a man really hears
the Gospel, his whole life must be reassessed, if he is sincere, for the
demands of Christ do not countenance half measures.

*How blest you are, when you suffer insults and persecution and every
kind of calumny for my sake. Accept it with gladness and exultation, for
you have a rich reward in heaven.* (Matt. 5, 11-12)

*You must not think that I have come to bring peace to the earth; I have
not come to bring peace, but a sword.* (Matt. 10, 34)

*If the world hates you, it hated me first, as you know well. If you
belonged to the world, the world would love its own; but because you do
not belong to the world, because I have chosen you out of the world, for
that reason the world hates you. Remember what I said: A servant is not
greater than his master. As they persecuted me, they will persecute you.*
(John 15, 18-20)

I heard a priest, one who lived the Gospel, preach the Gospel.
The humble, the poor, were carried away,
The prominent, the wealthy, were shocked.
And I thought that such preaching of the Gospel would soon
    frighten away many of those now filling the church, and
    attract those now shunning it.

It occurred to me that it is a bad sign for a follower of Christ
to be well thought of by conventional "Christians."
Rather, it would be better if we were singled out as crazy or
radical.
It would be better if they pursued us, signed petitions against us,
tried to get rid of us.

This evening, Lord, I am afraid.
I am afraid, for your Gospel is terrible.
It is easy to hear it preached,
It is relatively easy not to be shocked by it,
But it is very difficult to live it.

I am afraid of deluding myself, Lord.
I am afraid of being satisfied with my decent little life,
I am afraid of my good habits, for I take them for virtues;
I am afraid of my little efforts, for I take them for progress;
I am afraid of my activities; they make me think I am giving
myself.
I am afraid of my clever planning; I take it for success.
I am afraid of my influence, I imagine that it will transform lives;
I am afraid of what I give; it hides what I withhold;
I am afraid, Lord; there are people who are poorer than I;
Not so well-educated,
housed,
heated,
fed,
cared for,
loved.
I am afraid, Lord, for I do not do enough for them,
I do not do everything for them.

I should give everything,
I should give everything till there is not a single pain, a single
misery, a single sin in the world.
I should then give all, Lord, all the time.
I should give my life.

Lord, it is not true, is it?
It is not true for everyone,
I am exaggerating, I must be sensible!

Son, there is only *one* commandment,
For *everyone*:
You shall love with *all* your heart,
            with *all* your soul,
            with *all* your strength.

Stages of the Road

These prayers are not a spiritual treatise on the
Christian life. They merely describe striking milestones
in the lives of many committed Christians.
A collection of their expressions, their words, is illuminating,
and may help others in communicating with God.
The first prayers are easy to grasp,
but it is not through the mind that the last can be understood.
It is only through life. Those who haven't gone
through these stages will smile at the simplicity of the words,
but all those who have, will relive in them
their own experience.
More prayers might have been written, but they
would have meaning for only a few. It is enough to know
that when a man has decided to make room in his life for God
and his fellow-men, the Lord never ceases to teach him
and help him to rise above himself.

Lord,
deliver me from myself

There are men who are their own victims, more miserable than
one can imagine because they are condemned to loving no one but
themselves. One must understand their suffering to free them, for
this suffering is nothing less than experiencing hell. If they find a
friend who brings them to the realization that they are their own
tormentors, it is the first step in their salvation, especially if they
find a committed Christian who is to them the light and joy that
can draw them away from themselves.

Perhaps then they will pray 'Lord, deliver me from myself.' If
they ask this earnestly, they are on the road to salvation. This is the
first stage.

We too can say this prayer every night when we come home to
escape men and God.

*As he was starting out on a journey, a stranger ran up, and kneeling before
him, asked, Good Master, what must I do to win eternal life?
. . . Jesus looked straight at him; his heart warmed to him, and he said,
One thing you lack: go, sell everything you have, and give to the poor,
and you will have riches in heaven; and come, follow me. At these words
his face fell and he went away with a heavy heart; for he was a man of
great wealth.* (Mark 10, 17, 21, 22)

Lord, do you hear me?

I'm suffering dreadfully.
Locked in myself,
Prisoner of myself,
I hear nothing but my voice,
I see nothing but myself,
And behind me there is nothing but suffering.
Lord, do you hear me?

Deliver me from my body; it is nothing but hunger, with its thousands of tentacles outstretched to appease its insatiable appetite.

Lord, do you hear me?

Deliver me from my heart; when I think that it's overflowing with love, I realize angrily that it is again myself that I love through the loved one.

Lord, do you hear me?

Deliver me from my mind, it is full of itself, of its ideas, its opinions; it cannot carry on a dialogue, as no words reach it but its own.

Alone, I am bored,
    I am weary,
      I hate myself,
      I am disgusted with myself.
For ages I have been turning around inside myself like a sick man in his feverish bed.

Everything seems dark, ugly, horrid.
It's because I can look only through myself.
I feel ready to hate men and the whole world.
It's because I'm disappointed that I cannot love them.
I would like to get away,
Walk, run, to another land.
I know that *joy* exists, I have seen it on singing faces.
I know that *light* exists, I have seen it in radiant eyes.
But, Lord, I cannot get away, for I love my prison and I hate it,
For my prison is myself,
And I love myself, Lord.
I both love and loathe myself.

Lord, I can no longer find my own door.
I grope around blindly,
I knock against my own walls, my own boundaries.
I hurt myself,
I am in pain,

Three
books

🍃🍃🍃

by
Michel
Quoist

michel quoist
THE CHRISTIAN RESPONSE

michel quoist
PRAYERS OF LIFE

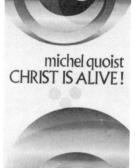

michel quoist
CHRIST IS ALIVE!

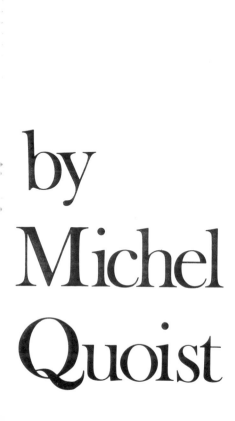

Christ is Alive!

An examination of the basic teachings of Christianity. Michel Quoist's concern is to make relevant to modern men and women the basic timelessness of the Christian message.   75p

The Christian Response

A series of practical contemporary meditations. The author never loses sight of man's humanity nor of the fact that the only way to heaven is earth.   80p

Prayers of Life

This book has been accepted by Christians of all denominations as fulfilling the widespread need for a book which would help them to pray as relevantly as they try to live. Over a quarter of a million copies have been sold in the English language edition.

"If only Abbé Quoist and his like had appeared before. His total commitment and deep compassion cannot fail to move anyone who is not spiritually dead. But don't buy this book unless you are prepared for a spiritual knockout."—*Baptist Times.*   60p

Also available in rexine binding   £1.50

ORDER FORM

To (Bookseller)

Please supply

.... copies CHRIST IS ALIVE! 75p

.... copies THE CHRISTIAN RESPONSE 80p

.... copies PRAYERS OF LIFE 60p

.... copies PRAYERS OF LIFE (Rexine) £1.50

Name...

Address ....

Gill and Macmillan, Publishers, 2 Belvedere Place, Dublin 1.

I am in too much pain, and no one knows it, for no one has come in.
I am alone, all alone.

Lord, Lord, do you hear me?
Lord, show me my door,
     take me by the hand.
Open the door,
Show me the way,
The path leading to *joy,* to *light.*

. . . But . . .
But, Lord, do you hear me?

Son, I have heard you.
I am sorry for you.
I have long been watching your closed shutters; open them,
     my light will come in.
I have long been standing at your locked door; open it, you will
     find me on the threshold.
I am waiting for you, the others are waiting for you,
But you must open,
You must come out.

Why choose to be a prisoner of yourself?
You are free.·
It is not I who locked the door,
It is not I who can open it.
. . . For it is you, from the inside, who persist in keeping it solidly
     barred.

Lord,
why did you tell me to love?

He who has begun to give himself to others is saved. In receiving his neighbour he will receive God and will be freed from himself. We are our own most deadly enemy. Humanly speaking we bring suffering on ourselves, and supernaturally we bar the road to God. There are men who are bent on refining themselves. They examine themselves, spend their time combating their faults, and never get beyond themselves, except sometimes to cultivate little hot-house virtues cut to their own size. They are wrong. Certain educators encourage them in this course, not realizing that by pointing out such and such a fault to conquer, such and such a quality to acquire, they centre their attention on themselves and condemn them to stagnation. No, one should study men carefully to find out, first, not what is bad in them, but what is good, to discover their potentialities. Next, study in detail their environment and help them to become an integral part of it by giving themselves to others.

All men can and must give themselves. If they have one talent, let them give that; if they have ten, let them give the ten. It's only in giving that one can receive.

But anyone who has begun this giving realizes very quickly, if he is honest, that he can't retreat. He is afraid: one must then encourage him, show him that it's only on the condition that he gives to others that he will succeed in his life and will know the joy of God.

A long time afterwards their master returned, and proceeded to settle accounts with them. The man who had been given the five bags of gold came and produced the five he had made: Master, he said, you left five bags with me; look, I have made five more. Well done, my good and trusty servant! said the master. You have proved trustworthy in a small way; I will now put you in charge of something big. Come and share your master's delight. (Matt. 25, 19-21)

It is by this that we know what love is: that Christ laid down his life for us. And we in our turn are bound to lay down our lives for our brothers. But if a man has enough to live on, and yet when he sees his brother in need shuts his heart against him, how can it be said that the divine love dwells in him? My children, love must not be a matter of words or talk; it must be genuine, and show itself in action. This is how we may know that we belong to the realm of truth. (I John 3, 16-19)

Lord, why did you tell me to love all men, my brothers?
I have tried, but I come back to you, frightened . . .
Lord, I was so peaceful at home, I was so comfortably settled.
It was well furnished, and I felt cozy.
I was alone, I was at peace,
Sheltered from the wind, the rain, the mud.
I would have stayed unsullied in my ivory tower.
But, Lord, you have discovered a breach in my defences,
You have forced me to open my door,
Like a squall of rain in the face, the cry of men has awakened me;
Like a gale of wind a friendship has shaken me,
As a ray of light slips in unnoticed, your grace has stirred me
. . . and, rashly enough, I left my door ajar. Now, Lord, I am lost!
Outside men were lying in wait for me.
I did not know they were so near; in this house, in this street,
      in this office; my neighbour, my colleague, my friend.
As soon as I started to open the door I saw them, with out-
      stretched hands, burning eyes, longing hearts, like beggars
      on church steps.

The first ones came in, Lord. There was after all some space in my
      heart.
I welcomed them. I would have cared for them and fondled them,
      my very own little lambs, my little flock.
You would have been pleased, Lord, I would have served and
      honoured you in a proper, respectable way.
Till then, it was sensible . . .
But the next ones, Lord, the other men, I had not seen them;
      they were hidden behind the first ones.
There were more of them, they were wretched; they over-
      powered me without warning.
We had to crowd in, I had to find room for them.
Now they have come from all over, in successive waves, pushing
      one another, jostling one another.

They have come from all over town, from all parts of the country,
    of the world; numberless, inexhaustible.
They don't come alone any longer but in groups, bound one to
    another.
They come bending under heavy loads; loads of injustice, of
    resentment and hate, of suffering and sin . . .
They drag the world behind them, with everything rusted,
    twisted, or badly adjusted.

Lord, they hurt me! They are in the way, they are everywhere.
They are too hungry, they are consuming me!
I can't do anything any more; as they come in, they push the
    door, and the door opens wider . . .
Lord! my door is wide open!
I can't stand it any more! It's too much! It's no kind of a life!
What about my job?
        my family?
        my peace?
        my liberty?
        and me?
Lord, I have lost everything, I don't belong to myself any longer;
There's no more room for me at home.

Don't worry, God says, you have gained all.
While men came in to you,
I, your Father,
I, your God,
Slipped in among them.

Help me to say "Yes"

Marked by the joy of his first self-giving, the committed Christian can no longer retreat. Aroused by love, his emotions have helped him to surmount all obstacles. He is swept along, pushed along by those whose demands become more and more pressing. And now God appears, no longer hidden behind men, but in full light. He asks to be received and given first place in man's life and activities. The Christian who has recognized him often runs away, for he knows that God will ask of him total and unconditional self-giving. Relentlessly the Lord pursues him to get the consent which will make his life divine.

Only those who have experienced this 'wrestling' with God can really understand this prayer: 'Help me to say "yes".'

A painful stage; the educator, the friend must understand it. Tactful—not to hinder God, for he has himself just undertaken the training of his son—but there to enlighten through faith where needed. Helping him to recognize the Lord, interpreting the questions that love asks constantly through the events of life, pointing out his invitations, his advances, his wooing; he must encourage the Christian and urge him to say 'yes.' If it hurts, it is because of his resistance; he must be helped to discover this. For one is always the loser when one battles with God. He is the stronger. His *love* is the stronger.

Into her presence the angel came, and said, Hail, thou who art full of grace; the Lord is with thee; . . . She was much perplexed at hearing him speak so, and cast about in her mind, what she was to make of such a greeting. Then the angel said to her, Mary, do not be afraid; thou hast found favour in the sight of God. And behold, thou shalt conceive in thy womb, and shalt bear a son, and shalt call him Jesus. He shall be great, and men will know him for the son of the most high; . . . nothing can be impossible with God. And Mary said, Behold the handmaid of the Lord; let it be unto me according to thy word. (Luke 1, 28-38)

I am afraid of saying 'yes,' Lord.
Where will you take me?
I am afraid of drawing the longer straw,
I am afraid of signing my name to an unread agreement,
I am afraid of the 'yes' that entails other 'yeses.'
And yet I am not at peace.
You pursue me, Lord, you besiege me.
I run after noise for fear of hearing you, but in a moment of silence
you slip through.
I turn from the road, for I have caught sight of you, but at the
end of the path you are there awaiting me.
Where shall I hide? I meet you everywhere.
Is it then impossible to escape you?

But I am afraid to say 'yes,' Lord.
I am afraid of putting my hand in yours, for you hold on to it.
I am afraid of meeting your eyes, for you can win me.
I am afraid of your demands, for you are a jealous God.
I am hemmed in, yet I hide.
I am captured, yet I struggle, and I fight knowing that I am
defeated.
For you are the stronger, Lord, you own the world and you take it
from me.
When I stretch out my hand to catch hold of people and things,
they vanish before me.
It's no fun, Lord, I can't keep anything for myself,
The flower I pick fades in my hands.
My laugh freezes on my lips.
The waltz I dance leaves me restless and uneasy.
Everything seems empty,
Everything seems hollow,
You have made a desert around me.
I am hungry and thirsty,
And the whole world cannot satisfy me.
And yet I loved you, Lord; what have I done to you?
I worked for you; I gave myself for you.
O great and terrible God,
What more do you want?

Son, I want more for you and for the world.
Until now you have planned your actions,
    but I have no need for them.

You have asked for my approval, you have asked for my support,
    you have wanted to interest me in your work.
But don't you see, son, that you were reversing the roles.
I have watched you, I have seen your good-will,
And I want more than you, now.
You will no longer do your own works, but the will of your
    Father in Heaven.

Say 'yes,' son.
I need your 'yes' as I needed Mary's 'yes' to come to earth,
For it is I who must do your work,
It is I who must live in your family,
It is I who must be in your neighbourhood,
    and not you.
For it is my look that penetrates, and not yours,
My words that carry weight, and not yours,
My life that transforms, and not yours.
Give all to me, abandon all to me.
I need your 'yes' to be united with you and to come down to earth,
I need your 'yes' to continue saving the world!

O Lord, I am afraid of your demands, but who can resist you?
That your Kingdom may come and not mine,
That your will may be done and not mine,
Help me to say *yes*.

Nothing, I am nothing

Man does not know himself. No matter how carefully he examines his conscience, he finds there nothing very blameworthy. He is not humble. Try as he may to think poorly of himself, he never succeeds in destroying his self-esteem. At first the committed Christian, having left himself for others, finds success in his undertakings, and gives himself credit for it. But in so doing he hinders God. It is only when man is deeply aware of his utter helplessness, that God can begin to accomplish all. Fortunately, when man effaces himself to make room for his brothers, God enters, and with him, his light. In this light he sees himself and the tiniest threads of his actions. He no longer needs to tell himself that it is God who directs his actions and makes them effective—*he knows it.* The Christian must be urged not to shy away from this painful revelation, not to be discouraged, for this experience is a God-given grace, without which he would never have known the greatness of God and the smallness of man. May he never forget it.

I am the vine, you are its branches; if a man lives on in me, and I in him, then he will yield abundant fruit; separated from me, you have no power to do anything. (John 15, 5; Knox)

Believe me when I tell you this; the man who has learned to believe in me will be able to do what I do; . . . and whatever request you make of the Father in my name, I will grant, so that through the Son the Father may be glorified. (John 14, 12-13; Knox)

Lord, you wanted it, here I am on the ground.
I don't even dare rise, I don't even dare look at you.
Nothing, I am nothing, I know it now.
Your light is terrible, Lord, and I'd like to escape it.

Since I have accepted you, you have bared my dwelling.
Every day, mercilessly, your light uncovers it,
And I see what I had never seen before.

I see the forest of my sins behind the tree that hid them.
I see innumerable roots, impossible to grasp,
I see that everything in me is an obstacle to you, as the smallest
    particle of matter blocks the sunlight and brings on the night.
I see the devil attacking the key-points of the fortress that I
    thought impregnable, and I find myself tottering and ready
    to fall.
I see my helplessness, I who thought that I could make myself
    of value to you.
I see that everything in me is mixed, and that not one of my actions
    is pure.
I see the infinite depth of each fault in the face of your infinite love.
I feel incapable of reaching a single soul, through the noise of my
    words and the wind of my gestures.
I see the Spirit blow where I haven't toiled, and the grain take
    root where I haven't sown.

Nothing, I am nothing, I accomplish nothing, I know it now.
Your light is hard, merciless, Lord.
No corner of my life and soul remains in the shadow.
Turn as I may, your light is everywhere,
And I stand naked and full of fear.

Formerly, I admitted that I was a sinner, that I was unworthy,
And I believed it, Lord, but I didn't know it.
In your presence I looked for some faults
But produced only laboured and feeble confessions.
Lord, it's my whole being that kneels now,
It's the sin that I am that asks forgiveness.

Lord, thank you for your light—I would never have known.
But, Lord, enough. I assure you I've understood.
I am *nothing*
And you are *all*.

Agony:
Lord, I am crushed

The day will come when the committed Christian will experience a violent encounter with evil. In a few hours its depth and extent may be revealed to him. As he cannot communicate his secret to others, he will carry, crushed and alone, in revulsion and darkness, the evil he thought he knew, but of which he had seen only the fringes. This deep contact with the sin of the world is the first step in a trial which is essential to his purification and to the deepening of his redemptive mission. This dark night will later settle in his innermost soul, but it will be the dawn of the resurrection.

Christ never knew sin, and God made him into sin for us, so that in him we might be turned into the holiness of God. (II Cor. 5, 21; Knox)

And now he grew dismayed and distressed: My soul, he said to them, is ready to die with sorrow; do you abide here, and keep watch. So he went forward a little, and fell on the ground, and prayed that if it were possible, the hour might pass him by: Abba, Father, he said, all things are possible to thee; take away this chalice from before me; only as thy will is, not as mine is. (Mark 14, 33-36; Knox)

And now my soul is distressed. What am I to say? I will say, Father, save me from undergoing this hour of trial; and yet, I have only reached this hour of trial that I might undergo it. Father, make thy name known. (John 12, 27, 28; Knox)

Lord, I am sickened,
     I am crushed tonight.
Sin is horrible, Lord,
     it is ugly,
     it is dirty.

I have walked in mud,
    travelled in mud,
        wallowed in mud.

The world is mud.
I feel that I must wash
    my hands,
    my eyes,
    my body,
    my heart,
    my soul,
    everything, Lord.
I've lost courage to go forward,
I hardly dare look at myself.
Why did you show me sin, why did you make me understand it?
I can never forget it.
I feel so old tonight, older than my deceptive face.
In a few hours I have aged ten years.

Forgive me, Lord, I did not know.
Forgive the happy people, the sinless people, the pure, the
    innocent, who cannot understand, who will never know or
    suspect what sin is.
How hideous it is, Lord!

There is a picture before me: the smiling and honest face of a
    big boy. And it both quiets and revolts me.
I envy him his innocence and I resent his calm.
I am drawn to his smile, yet it hurts me.
I crave his untarnished purity, yet it wounds me.
Lord, how know sin and yet remain pure?
How know, and be at peace?
How carry the infinite sadness of sin and keep within me your
    profound joy?

Son, you must accept this evil on your road;
    you must even carry it.
Don't stop, but seize it in passing;
    it's for this that I sent you treading these roads.
It crushes you. You can no longer go forward. You collapse,
    revolted, in the dark, alone.

I know this,
I have experienced this, son.
That was my agony.
One must go through this, it's the law of my redemption.
For before rising one must die,
    and before dying one must suffer.
Don't run from evil; on the contrary, be present. Take hold of it.
The uglier it is, the heavier it is, the more you must grasp it;
    and suffer,
    and die.
    Joy will follow.

Temptation

When a Christian has chosen to live for God and for others, the devil is not pleased. At certain times the din of temptation, covered for a while by the song of love, returns more strident than ever.

God allows this trial, and is sometimes even deaf to the appeals of his child, in order to test him and to bring him to greater trust. Only when the Christian expects nothing of himself and everything of God, can he be at peace.

One must be very little to be carried by God.

So he took ship, and his disciples followed him. And suddenly a great storm arose on the sea, so that the waves rose high over the ship; but he lay asleep. And his disciples came and roused him, crying, Lord, save us, we are sinking. But Jesus said to them, Why are you faint-hearted, men of little faith? Then he rose up, and checked the winds, and the sea, and there was deep calm. (Matt. 8, 23-26; Knox)

Believe me, unless you become like little children again, you shall not enter the kingdom of heaven. (Matt. 18, 3; Knox)

I'm at the end of my tether, Lord.
I am shattered,
I am broken.
Since this morning I have been struggling to escape temptation,
      which, now subtle, now persuasive, now tender, now
         sensuous, dances before me like a glamour girl at a fair.
I don't know what to do.
I don't know where to go.
It spies on me, follows me, engulfs me.
When I leave a room I find it seated and waiting for me in the next.

When I seize a newspaper, there it is, hidden in the words of a
    harmless story;
I go out, and see it smiling at me on an unknown face,
I turn away and look at the wall, and it leaps at me from a poster.
I return to work, to find it dozing on my files, and when I gather
    my papers, it awakens.
In despair, I take my poor head in my hands, I shut my eyes to
    see nothing,
But I discover that it is more alive than ever, comfortably settled
    within me.
For it has broken my door open, it has slipped into my body,
    my veins,
    to the very tips of my fingers.
It has seeped into the crevices of my memory
And sings into the ear of my imagination.
It plays on my nerves as on the strings of a guitar.
I don't know where I stand, Lord.
I don't know whether or not I want this sin that beckons to me.
I no longer know whether I pursue it or am pursued.
I am dizzy, and the void draws me as it draws the rash mountaineer
    who can neither advance nor retreat.
Lord, Lord, help me!

Son, I am here.
I haven't left you.
How weak is your faith!

You are too proud.
You still rely on yourself.
If you want to surmount all temptations, without falling or
    weakening, calm and serene,
You must surrender yourself to me.
You must realize that you are neither big enough nor strong
    enough,
You must let yourself be guided like a child,
My little child.
Come, give me your hand, and do not fear.
If there is mud, I will carry you in my arms.
But you must be very, very little,
For the Father carries only little children.

Sin

It is not only temptation that tries the generous Christian, but at times sin also; he may have a heavy fall, one that he had thought impossible, so deep and strong had seemed his love for the Lord. And having fallen, he is likely to become discouraged. Never before has he understood to such an extent the ugliness of sin—it's because he has now a greater understanding of the love of God. All is grace. This fall will make him realize that he cannot rely on himself at all. It will put him in his place—at the bottom. But with this mistrust of himself must go a greater confidence in God, the Father.

And indeed, for fear that these surpassing revelations should make me proud, I was given a sting to distress my outward nature, an angel of Satan sent to rebuff me. Three times it made me entreat the Lord to rid me of it; but he told me, My grace is enough for thee; my strength finds its full scope in thy weakness . . . when I am weakest, then I am strongest of all. (II Cor. 12, 7-10)
So it is, I tell you, in heaven; there will be more rejoicing over one sinner who repents, than over ninety-nine souls that are justified, and have no need of repentance. (Luke 15, 7)

I have fallen, Lord,
Once more.
I can't go on, I'll never succeed.
I am ashamed, I don't dare look at you.
And yet I struggled, Lord, for I knew you were right near me,
      bending over me, watching.
But temptation blew like a hurricane
And instead of looking at you I turned my head away,
I stepped aside
While you stood, silent and sorrowful,
Like the spurned fiancé who sees his loved one carried off by his
      rival.

When the wind died down as suddenly as it had arisen,
When the lightning ceased after proudly streaking the darkness,
All of a sudden I found myself alone, ashamed, disgusted, with
    my sin in my hands.

This sin that I selected as a customer his purchase,
This sin that I have paid for and cannot return, for the store-
    keeper is no longer there,
This tasteless sin,
This odourless sin,
This sin that sickens me,
That I have wanted but want no more,
That I have imagined,
           sought,
           played with,
           fondled,
           for a long time,
That I have finally embraced while coldly by-passing you,
My arms outstretched, my eyes and heart irresistibly drawn;
This sin that I have grasped and consumed with gluttony,
It's mine now, but it possesses me as the spider-web holds captive
    the fly.
It is mine,
It sticks to me,
It flows in my veins,
It fills my heart.
It has slipped in everywhere, as darkness slips into the forest at
    dusk and fills all the patches of light.

I can't get rid of it.
I run from it, like the master of an unwanted and mangy dog,
    but it catches up with me, and rubs joyfully against my legs.
Everyone must notice it.
I'm so ashamed that I feel like crawling to avoid being seen,
I'm ashamed of being seen by my friend,
I'm ashamed of being seen by you, Lord,
For you loved me, and I forgot you.
I forgot you because I was thinking of myself,
And one can't think of several persons at once.
One must choose, and I chose.

And your voice,
And your look,
And your love hurt me.
They weigh me down,
They weigh me down more than my sin.

Lord, don't look at me like that,
For I am naked,
I am dirty,
I am down,
Shattered,
With no strength left.
I dare make no more promises,
I can only stand bowed before you.

Come, son, look up.
Isn't it mainly your vanity that is wounded?
If you loved me, you would grieve, but you would trust.
Do you think that there's a limit to God's love?
Do you think that for a moment I stopped loving you?
But you still rely on yourself, son.
You must rely only on me.

Ask my pardon
And get up quickly.
You see, it's not falling that is the worst,
But staying on the ground.

It is dark

It is only one totally blind who puts himself completely into the hands of God, to be led like a child. So, to raise the service of the Christian above the human level, the Lord is obliged to plunge him into darkness. He then learns to rely on God only.

He once had great faith in organized activities, and now he no longer knows what course to take. He once believed in the effectiveness of his words, and now he can no longer express himself. He once valued meetings, and now those he has carefully prepared fail dismally. Where he had met only with success, he now encounters only reverses. And God, seeming to make fun of his sudden and total ineffectiveness, acts along channels of his own without the help of this 'useless servant.' When the Christian, ashamed and in despair, turns to Christ to weep, he no longer finds him.

This is a painful time. The Christian mustn't try to escape it, but he does need to be reassured.

As the dam checks the flow of water to raise its level and unchain its power, so God, through outward failure, raises his disciple above the plane of mediocrity to a transcendence of self by faith.

When the sixth hour came, there was darkness over all the earth until the ninth hour; and at the ninth hour Jesus cried out with a loud voice, . . . My God, my God, why hast thou forsaken me? (Mark 15, 33-35; Knox)

Lord, it is dark.
Lord, are you here in my darkness?

Your light has gone out, and so has its reflection on men and on all things around me.

Everything seems grey and sombre as when a fog blots out the
    sun and enshrouds the earth.
Everything is an effort, everything is difficult, and I am heavy-
    footed and slow.
Every morning I am overwhelmed at the thought of another day.
I long for the end, I yearn for the oblivion of death.
I should like to leave,
    run away,
    flee,
    anywhere, escape.
Escape what?
You, Lord, others, myself, I don't know,
But leave,
Flee.

I progress haltingly like a drunkard
From force of habit, unconsciously.
I go through the same motions each day, but I know that they
    are meaningless.
I walk, but I know that I get nowhere.
I speak, and my words seem dreadfully empty, for they can reach
    only human ears and not the living souls who are far above.
Ideas themselves escape me, and I find it hard to think.
I stammer, confused, blushing,
And I feel ridiculous and abashed, for people will notice me.
Lord, am I losing my mind?
Or is all this what you want?

It wouldn't matter, except that I am alone.
I am alone.
You have taken me far, Lord; trusting, I followed you, and you
    walked at my side,
And now, at night, in the middle of the desert, suddenly you have
    disappeared.
I call, and you do not answer.
I search, and I do not find you.
I have left everything, and now am left alone.
Your absence is my suffering.

Lord, it is dark.
Lord, are you here in my darkness?

Where are you, Lord?
Do you love me still?
Or have I wearied you?
Lord, answer,
Answer!

It is dark.

Lord, you have seized me

The Christian who has 'capitulated' to the Lord, who has said 'Yes,' often receives his reward immediately. The Lord gives him the *joy* of possessing him and of being possessed by him.

Words are inadequate to describe this loving embrace of God. The boy who is 'seized' by his Master right in the middle of the traffic, and has to dismount from his bicycle—suddenly unable to go on safely—will understand. So will the young girl who has to leave the workroom abruptly to hide from her companions her transfigured face. Also the boy who innocently confesses that he has to beg God to 'leave him for a while' at a gathering in order to be available to his friends.

Though we must not seek these perceptible graces, we must be simple enough to thank the Lord when he grants them to us, enjoying his tenderness before experiencing his uncompromising firmness.

We have learned to recognize the love God has in our regard, to recognize it, and to make it our belief. God is love; that love resides, not in our shewing any love for God, but in his shewing love for us first. (I John 4, 16, 10; Knox)

And all this, which once stood to my credit, I now write down as loss, for the love of Christ. For that matter, there is nothing I do not write down as loss compared with the high privilege of knowing Christ Jesus, my Lord; for love of him I have lost everything, treat everything else as refuse, if I may have Christ to my credit . . . I only press on, in hope of winning the mastery, as Christ Jesus has won the mastery over me. (Phil. 3; 7, 8, 12; Knox)

Lord, you seized me and I could not resist you.
I ran for a long time, but you followed me.
I took by-paths, but you knew them.

You overtook me.
I struggled,
You won.
Here I am, Lord, out of breath, no fight left in me, and I've said
'yes,' almost unwillingly.
When I stood there trembling like one defeated before his captor,
Your look of love fell on me.

The die is cast, Lord, I can no longer forget you.
In a moment you seized me,
In a moment you conquered me.
My doubts were swept away,
My fears dispelled.
For I recognized you without seeing you.
I felt you without touching you,
I understood you without hearing you.

Marked by the fire of your love, I can no longer forget you.
Now I know that you are there, close to me, and I work in
peace beneath your loving gaze.
I no longer know what it is to make an effort to pray.
I just lift my eyes to you and I meet yours.
And we understand one another. All is light, all is peace.

At times, O Lord, you steal over me irresistibly, as the ocean
slowly covers the shore,
Or suddenly you seize me as the lover clasps his beloved in his
arms.
And I am helpless, a prisoner, and I have to stand still.
Captivated, I hold my breath, the world fades away, you suspend
time.
I wish that these minutes were hours . . .
When you withdraw, leaving me afire and overwhelmed with
profound joy,
Though I have no new ideas, I *know* that you possess me more
completely.
You have reached new depths in me,
The wound has widened and I am more than ever a prisoner of
your love.
Lord, once more you have made a desert around me, but this
time it is different.

You are too great, you eclipse everything.
What I had cherished now seems trifling, and my desires melt
    like wax in the sun under the fire of your love.
Nothing matters to me,
Neither my comfort
Nor even my life.
I desire only you,
I want nothing but you.

I know that the others say, 'He is mad!'
But, Lord, it is they who are out of their minds.
They do not know you, they do not know God, they do not know
    that one cannot resist him.
But you have seized me, Lord, and I am sure of you.
You are there, and I am overjoyed.
Sunlight floods over all, and my life shines like a jewel.
How easy everything is, how luminous!
All is pure and joyful.

Thank you, Lord, thank you!
Why me, why did you choose me?
Joy, joy, tears of joy.

Before you, Lord

Words, ideas, mental images are needed to nourish the beginner's prayers; but, little by little, he finds that all these props are obstacles in reaching God. Christ, when he takes hold of his disciple, makes him understand that it is useless for him to say or imagine or think anything at all. He must let God work in him. To expose oneself to him without intermediary is the surest way of meeting him when he calls. Nevertheless, receptivity does not mean forgetfulness of men. On the contrary, the disciple, laden with the weight of the brothers he has taken into his keeping, must bring them silently to God—to make possible a meeting, with them, in his presence.

But when thou art praying, go into thy inner room and shut the door upon thyself, and so pray to thy Father in secret; and then thy Father, who sees what is done in secret, will reward thee.
Moreover, when you are at prayer, do not use many phrases. (Matt. 6, 6-7)
For my own part, I will gladly spend and be spent on your souls' behalf. (II Cor. 12, 15)
No nursing mother ever cherished her children more; in our great longing for you, we desired nothing better than to offer you our own lives, as well as God's gospel, so greatly had we learned to love you. (I Thess. 2, 7-8)

To be there before you, Lord, that's all.
To shut the eyes of my body,
To shut the eyes of my soul,
And be still and silent,
To expose myself to you who are there, exposed to me.
To be there before you, the Eternal Presence.

I am willing to feel nothing, Lord,
                    to see nothing,
                    to hear nothing.
Empty of all ideas,
        of all images,
In the darkness.
Here I am, simply,
To meet you without obstacles,
In the silence of faith,
Before you, Lord.

But, Lord, I am not alone
I can no longer be alone.
I am a crowd, Lord,
For men live within me.
I have met them.
They have come in,
They have settled down,
They have worried me,
They have tormented me,
They have devoured me.
And I have allowed it, Lord, that they might be nourished and
    refreshed.
I bring them to you, too, as I come before you.
I expose them to you in exposing myself to you.
Here I am,
Here they are,
Before you, Lord.

Prayers on
the Way of the Cross

*Christ is still dying. He continues to offer himself
to his Father for the redemption of the world
through the men who today suffer and die around us.
The Way of the Cross is also the way to life;
this a real Christian should never forget.*

1 *Jesus is condemned to death*

So it was, brethren, that when I came to you and preached Christ's message to you, I did so without any high pretensions to eloquence, or to philosophy. I had no thought of bringing you any other knowledge than that of Jesus Christ, and of him as crucified. It was with distrust of myself, full of anxious fear, that I approached you; my preaching, my message depended on no persuasive language, devised by human wisdom, but rather on the proof I gave you of spiritual power; God's power, not man's wisdom, was to be the foundation of your faith. (I Cor. 2, 1-5; Knox)

Lord, it's too late for you to be quiet, you have spoken too much; you have fought too much;

You were not sensible, you know, you exaggerated, it was bound to happen.

You called the better people a breed of vipers;

You told them that their hearts were black sepulchres with fine exteriors;

You kissed the decaying lepers;

You spoke fearlessly with unacceptable strangers;

You ate with notorious sinners, and you said that street-walkers would be the first in Paradise;

You got on well with the poor, the tramps, the crippled;

You belittled the religious regulations;

Your interpretation of the Law reduced it to one little commandment: to love.

Now they are avenging themselves.

They have taken steps against you; they have approached the authorities and action will follow.

Lord, I know that if I try to live a little like you, I shall be condemned.

I am afraid.

They are already singling me out.

Some smile at me, others laugh, some are shocked, and several
   of my friends are about to drop me.
I am afraid to stop,
I am afraid to listen to men's wisdom,
It whispers: you must go forward little by little, everything
   can't be taken literally, it's better to come to terms with the
   adversary . . .
And yet, Lord, I know that you are right.
Help me to fight,
Help me to speak,
Help me to live your Gospel,
To the end,
To the folly of the Cross.

2 Jesus bears his cross

If any man has a mind to come my way, let him renounce self, and take up his cross daily, and follow me. He who tries to save his life will lose it; it is the man who loses his life for my sake, that will save it. (Luke 9, 23-24)

Lord, here is your Cross.

Your Cross! As if it were your cross!
You had no cross and you came to get ours, and all through
      your life, and along the way to Calvary, you took upon you,
      one by one, the sins of the world.
You have to go forward,
And bend,
And suffer.
The Cross must be carried.

Lord, you walk on silently; is it true then that there is a time
      for speaking and a time for silence?
Is it true that there is a time for struggling and another for the
      silent bearing of our sins and the sins of the world?

Lord, I would rather fight the Cross; to bear it is hard. The more I
      progress, and the more I see the evil in the world, the heavier
      is the Cross on my shoulders.
Lord, help me to understand that the most generous deed is
      nothing unless it is also silently redemptive.
And since you want this long way of the Cross for me,
At the dawning of each day, help me to set forth.

3 Jesus falls for the first time

Jesus said to them (Simon and Simon's brother Andrew), Come and follow me; I will make you into fishers of men. And they dropped their nets immediately, and followed him. (Mark 1, 17-18)
But Jesus said to them (James and John), Have you strength to drink of the cup I am to drink of, to be baptized with the baptism I am to be baptized with? They said to him, We have. (Mark 10, 38-39)
But he took Peter and James and John with him. And now he grew dismayed and distressed . . . Then he went back, and found them asleep; and he said to Peter, Simon, art thou sleeping? Hadst thou not strength to watch even for an hour? (Mark 14, 33-37)

He fell.
For a moment he staggered, then fell prostrate,
God in the dust.

And so, Lord, I followed you, setting out with confidence, and
     now I have fallen.
I thought I had given myself irrevocably to you, but I caught
     sight of a flower on a foot-path.
I left you, I left the cumbersome Cross, and here I am off the road,
     possessed of a few faded petals and my solitude.
And the others, Lord, pass along the road, broken, exhausted,
And crosses are in the making and backs are bending.
I am no longer there to fight evil and to help men to drag their
     loads.
I am off the road.
Lord, help me not only to follow after you but to keep steadily on.
Keep me from sudden weaknesses that leave me stupefied and
     empty, far from the place where you are shaping the world.

4 Jesus meets his mother

As for thy own soul, it shall have a sword to pierce it. (Luke 2, 35;
Knox)

Lord, I pity your poor Mother.
She follows,
She follows you,
She follows mankind on its Way of the Cross.

She walks in the crowd, unknown, but she doesn't take her eyes
    from you.
Every gesture of yours, every sigh, every blow, every wound,
    enters her heart.
She knows your sufferings,
She suffers your sufferings,
And without coming near you,
    without touching you,
    without speaking to you,
Lord, with you she saves the world.

Often, mingled with the crowd, I accompany men on their
    Way of the Cross,
And I am crushed by evil.
I feel incapable of saving the world; it is too heavy and rotten,
    and every day at the turn of the road I meet with new
    injustices and new impurities.

Lord, show me your Mother, Mary,
The useless one, the ineffectual one in the sight of men,
But the co-redemptrice in the sight of God.
Help me to walk among men, eager to know their miseries and
    their sins.
May I never avert my eyes.

May I never close my heart, that in welcoming the sufferings of the world, with Mary, your Mother, I may suffer and redeem.

5 Simon of Cyrene
helps to carry Jesus' cross

And led him away to be crucified. As for his cross, they forced a passer-by who was coming in from the country to carry it, one Simon of Cyrene. (Mark 15, 20-21)
Bear the burden of one another's failings; then you will be fulfilling the law of Christ. (Gal. 6, 2)

He passed by on the road;
They pressed him into service,
The first to come along, a stranger.

Lord, you accepted his help.
You did not want the help of a friend, the solace of a gesture
    of love, the generous impulse of one who cared.
You chose the enforced help of an indifferent and timid fellow.
Lord All-Powerful, you sought the help of a powerless man.
By your own choosing you are in need of us.

Lord, I need others.
The way of man is too hard to be trodden alone.
But I avoid the hands outstretched to help me,
I want to act alone,
I want to fight alone,
I want to succeed alone.
And yet beside me walks a friend, a spouse, a brother, a neighbour,
    a fellow-worker.
You have placed them near me, Lord, and too often I ignore them.
And yet it is together that we shall save the world.
Lord, even if they are requisitioned, grant that I may see, that
    I may accept, all the Simons on my road.

6 *A woman wipes the face of Jesus*

We carry about continually in our bodies the dying state of Jesus, so that the living power of Jesus may be manifested in our bodies too. (II Cor. 4, 10)
At present, we are looking at a confused reflection in a mirror; then, we shall see face to face. (I Cor. 13, 12)

For a long time, Lord, her eyes were on you;
She suffered from your suffering.
Unable to bear it any longer, she pushed the soldiers aside and
    wiped your face, with a cloth of fine linen.
Were your bleeding features imprinted on her cloth? Maybe.
In her heart, surely.

Lord, I need to contemplate you at great length, disinterestedly,
    as a little brother admires and loves his big brother.
For I want to resemble you; and for that I must first look at you.
If you want, I shall become a little like you, since friends who
    love each other become one.
But, Lord, too often I pass in front of you carelessly, or am
    bored when I stop and look at you.
And to others I must be a sad caricature of you.
Forgive my body, eager for pleasures; it does not bring your
    presence to others.
Forgive my clouded eyes: in them others cannot see your light.
Forgive my encumbered heart: in it others do not see your love.

Nevertheless, Lord, come to me; my door is open.

7 Jesus falls for the second time

They all grew drowsy, and fell asleep. (Matt. 25, 5)
Only look well to yourselves; do not let your hearts grow dull ... Keep watch, then, praying at all times, so that you may be found worthy to come safe through all that lies before you, and stand erect to meet the presence of the Son of Man. (Luke 21, 34-36)

Lord, you are spent.
Again you have fallen to the ground.
This time, you fall not only from the weight of the Cross, but from exhaustion.

Recurrent suffering dulls the will.
My sins, Lord, are dulling my conscience.
I get used to evil very quickly:
A little self-indulgence here,
A small unfaithfulness there,
An unwise action farther on,
And my vision becomes obscured; I no longer see stumbling-blocks, I no longer see other people on my road,
My ears gradually close; I no longer hear the complaints of men.
I find myself on the ground, on the plain, far from the road you laid out for me.

Lord, I beseech you, keep me young in my efforts,
Spare me the bondage of habit, which lulls to sleep and kills.

8 Jesus rebukes the daughters of Jerusalem

How is it that thou canst see the speck of dust which is in thy brother's eye, and art not aware of the beam which is in thy own? By what right wilt thou say to thy brother, Brother, let me rid thy eye of that speck, when thou canst not see the beam that is in thy own? Thou hypocrite, take the beam out of thy own eye first, and so thou shalt have clear sight to rid thy brother's of the speck. (Luke 6, 41-42)

They weep.
They sob.
It's easy to understand if you see what men have done to him.
And they are powerless, they cannot interfere,
So they weep, they weep in pity.

Lord, you have seen them, you have heard them.
But you said: 'Weep first for your sins.'

I manage very well, Lord, to pity your sufferings and the sufferings
  of the world.
But to weep for my own sins, that's another matter.
I'd rather bemoan those of others,
It's easier.
I'm well up on that; the whole world passes every day before
  my tribunal.
I've found plenty of guilt: in politics, economics, slums, alcohol,
  films, industry. I see it in many people: in *laissez-faire*
  Christians, in priests who don't understand a thing; and in
  many others, Lord, many others.
All in all, in just about the whole world, except me.

Lord, teach me that I am a sinner.

9 Jesus falls for the third time

Jesus said to him (Peter), Believe me, this night, before the cock crows, thou wilt thrice disown me. (Matt. 26, 34)
Peter was deeply moved when he was asked a third time, Dost thou love me? and said to him, Lord, thou knowest all things; thou canst tell that I love thee. (John 21, 17)

Again.
You do not move, for all the soldiers' beatings.
Lord, are you dead?
No, but utterly spent.
A minute of terrible anxiety.
But you begin again, just as you are, Lord, and walk on. One step,
        then another . . .
Lord, you have fallen a third time, but this time close to Calvary.

Again.
I fall every time.
I'll never get there.
But I've said that before, Lord, and please forgive me, for you
        were right with me, you were just testing my faith.
If I become discouraged, I am lost.
If I keep up the fight, I am saved.
For you fell a third time, but you had nearly reached Calvary.

10 *Jesus is stripped of his garments*

The time has come now for the Son of Man to achieve his glory. Believe me when I tell you this; a grain of wheat must fall into the ground and die, or else it remaïns nothing more than a grain of wheat; but if it dies, then it yields rich fruit. (John 12, 23-24)

You had nothing left but your own cloak;
You were fond of it, your Mother had woven it for you.
But this, too, had to go.
One thing only is necessary, Lord, your Cross.

Nothing comes now between you and the Cross,
You are going to be united forever,
And together you will save the world.

And so, Lord, I must give up all these trappings which hinder
    me and hide me from your sight.
This 'possessing' which stifles the 'being' in me and separates
    me from others.
Thus, Lord, little by little everything in my life which is not
    an expression of your will must die.

I don't like it, Lord. It's always a question of dying!
How demanding you are!
I give, and you want more.
I'd like to keep a few trifles,
A few trifles I cling to, and can't bring myself to offer you.

But if you want all, Lord, take all.
Strip me, yourself, of my last garment.
For I well know that we must die to deserve life,
As the seed must die to turn into the golden grain.

11 *Jesus is nailed to the cross*

*With Christ I hang upon the cross, and yet I am alive; or rather, not I;
it is Christ that lives in me. True, I am living, here and now, this mortal
life; but my real life is the faith I have in the Son of God, who loved me,
and gave himself for me.* (Gal. 2, 19-20)

Lord, you stretch at full length on the Cross.
There.
Without a doubt, it is made for you.
You cover it entirely, and to adhere to it more surely,
    you allow men to nail you carefully to it.
Lord, it was work well done, conscientiously done.
Now you fit your Cross exactly, as the mechanic's carefully filed
    parts fit the engineer's blueprint.
There had to be this precision.

Thus, Lord, I must gather my body, my heart, my spirit,
And stretch myself at full length on the Cross of the present
    moment.
I haven't the right to choose the wood of my passion.
The Cross is ready, to my measure.
You present it to me each day, each minute, and I must lie on it.
It isn't easy. The present moment is so limited that there is no
    room to turn around.
And yet, Lord, I can meet you nowhere else.
It's there that you await me.
It's there that together we shall save our brothers.

12 Jesus dies on the cross

He dispossessed himself, and took the nature of a slave, fashioned in the likeness of men, and presenting himself to us in human form; and then he lowered his own dignity, accepted an obedience which brought him to death, death on a cross. (Phil. 2, 7-8; Knox)
We too must be ready to lay down our lives for the sake of our brethren. (I John 3, 16; Knox)

A few hours more,
A few minutes more,
A few instants more.
For thirty-three years it has been going on.
For thirty-three years you have lived fully minute after minute.
You can no longer escape, now; you are there, at the end of
     your life, at the end of your road.
You are at the last extremity, at the edge of a precipice.
You must take the last step,
The last step of love,
The last step of life that ends in death.

You hesitate.
Three hours are long, three hours of agony;
Longer than three years of life,
Longer than thirty years of life.

You must decide, Lord, all is ready around you.
You are there, motionless, on your Cross.
You have renounced all activity other than embracing these
     crossed planks for which you were made.
And yet, there is still life in your nailed body.
Let mortal flesh die, and make way for eternity.
Now, life slips from each limb, one by one, finding refuge in his
     still beating heart.

130

Immeasurable heart,
Overflowing heart,
Heart heavy as the world, the world of sins and miseries that it
    bears.

Lord, one more effort.
Mankind is there, waiting unknowingly for the cry of its Saviour.
Your brothers are there; they need you.
Your Father bends over you, already holding out his arms.
Lord, save us,
Save us.

See.
He has taken his heavy heart,
And,
Slowly,
Laboriously,
Alone between heaven and earth,
In the awesome night,
With passionate love,
He has gathered his life,
He has gathered the sin of the world,
And in a cry,
He has given *all*.
'Father, into thy hands I commit my spirit.'

Christ has just died for us.

Lord, help me to die for you.
Help me to die for them.

13 *Jesus is given to his mother*

And his mother said to him, My Son, why hast thou treated us so? Think,
what anguish of mind thy father and I have endured, searching for thee.
But he asked them, What reason had you to search for me? Could you not
tell that I must needs be about my Father's business? (Luke 2, 48-49;
Knox)

Your work is done,
You can leave your Cross,
You can come down to rest, you have surely earned it.

Slowly you slip down, like a man weary of labour and drowsy
  with sleep.
Your Mother takes you in her arms.
'What a state you are in; you were not sensible, you died of
  exhaustion!
Perhaps the Father did not require so much.'
But you rest in peace.
Over your face, calm and serene, there passes a ray of joy.
  All is accomplished.
You have made your Mother suffer, but she is proud of you.
'Sleep now, my little one, your Mother is watching you.'

Thus each night, my day ended, I fall asleep.
What a state I am in sometimes, Lord.
But, alas, it is not always in serving the Father that I have become
  soiled and tired.
Mary, will you be willing even so to watch over me every night?

My body is weighed down with its failures, but my heart asks
  forgiveness.
Don't forget, you are the refuge of sinners.
Holy Mary, Mother of God, pray for me, a poor sinner.

132

Grant that through the merits of your Son, I may never fall asleep
without receiving the forgiveness of our Father,
That, each night, resting in peace in your arms, I may learn how
to die.

14 *Jesus is laid in the tomb*

In this mortal frame of mine, I help to pay off the debt which the afflictions of Christ still leave to be paid, for the sake of his body, the church. (Col. 1, 24; Knox)
The sufferings of Christ, it is true, overflow into our lives; but there is overflowing comfort, too, which Christ brings to us. (II Cor. 1, 5; Knox)

Let's forget it now,
And all go home.
He is buried and the stone is in place.
His family is in tears, his friends are lost.
This time it is really over.

Lord, it is not over.
'You are in agony till the end of time,' I know.
Men tread the Way of the Cross in relays.
The resurrection will only be completed when they have reached
    the end of the way.
I am on the road; I have a small share of your suffering and the
    others have theirs.
Together we help you to carry the burden that you have assumed
    and made divine.
There lies my hope, Lord, and my invincible trust.
There is not a fraction of my little suffering that you have not
    already lived and transformed into infinite redemption.
When the road is hard and monotonous,
When it leads to the grave,
I know that beyond the grave you are waiting for me in your
    glory.
Lord, help me to travel along my road faithfully, at my proper
    place in the vast procession of humanity.

Help me above all to recognize you and to help you in all my
    pilgrim brothers.
For it would be a lie to weep before your lifeless image, if I did
    not follow you, living, on the road that men travel.